Our Naming of God

Our Naming of God

PROBLEMS AND PROSPECTS
OF GOD-TALK TODAY

Edited by Carl E. Braaten

Fortress Press
Minneapolis

OUR NAMING OF GOD
Problems and Prospects of God-Talk Today

Scripture quotations, unless otherwise noted, are from the Revised Standard Version of the Bible, copyright © 1946, 1952, and 1971 by the Division of Christian Education of the National Council of Churches.

Excerpt from *What's Bred in the Bone* by Robertson Davies. Copyright © 1985 by Robertson Davies. All rights reserved. Reprinted by permission of Viking Penguin Inc.

Cover design: Patricia M. Boman

Library of Congress Cataloging-in-Publication Data

Our naming of God.

   Bibliography: p.
   1. God—Name.   2. Languages—Religious aspects.
I. Braaten, Carl E., 1929–
BT180.N2095   1989   231'.014   88-16368
ISBN 0-8006-2301-0

The paper used in this publication meets the minimum requirements of American National Standard for Information Sciences—Permanence of Paper for Printed Library Materials, ANSI Z329.48-1984. ∞™

Manufactured in the U.S.A.   AF 1-2301

93   92   91   90   89   1   2   3   4   5   6   7   8   9   10

CONTENTS

PREFACE

*T*his book is the product of a year-long series of faculty seminars on the nature of God-language. For the past twenty years members of the faculty of the Lutheran School of Theology at Chicago have evolved a tradition of gathering on Monday afternoons from 3:45 to 5:00 for theological conversations, lubricated by appropriate libations and snacks. The discussions have usually focused on books or articles or other forms of theological expression generated out of faculty scholarship. Guest professors are always invited to participate and frequently lead the colloquium.

During the academic year of 1986–87 the faculty decided to change the formula and concentrate on a single theme for the entire year, meeting only once a month for two hours, in order to engage in an intensive, interdisciplinary investigation of problems associated with the timely theme of God-language. Our colleague Robert Bertram was appointed to be the coordinator of the faculty seminar series; he proposed the topics, selected the authors, and moderated the sessions. The overwhelming success of this unusual event in the common life of our faculty is in large part due to Robert Bertram's considerable skill in stimulating, shaping, and presiding over the process of our theological reflections. We owe him our thanks.

The topic of God-language was chosen by a faculty committee on scholarship and publication, which I chaired. In recent years the question of how to speak of God has broadened beyond academic circles to become a churchwide concern. In our own seminary community numerous forums have been held to discuss the gender issue posed by the feminist criticism of traditional patriarchal images that refer to God. The struggle for new God-language has been most acutely manifest in the context of corporate worship. Experiments at substituting feminine or neutral metaphors for male metaphors in a variety of liturgies, including the eucharistic service, have met with mixed reactions and sometimes stirred open and vigorous controversy. Hovering in the background, of course, was the ominous report from the Commission on the New Lutheran Church that it had defeated the motion—by just three votes—to exclude the triune name of God as Father, Son, and Holy Spirit from the

Constitution of the Evangelical Lutheran Church in America and put in its place their functional equivalents as Creator, Redeemer, and Sanctifier. This sent a scare throughout the church and in some way added to the urgency of the topic of God-language in our seminary community. Today the ideological motivation to proscribe the trinitarian naming of God, rooted in the Great Commission (Matt. 28:19-20), announced in every Christian's baptism and built into the ecumenical creeds, permeates every theological community, including our own. It may very well be that the triune name of God as Father, Son, and Holy Spirit is a matter of *status confessionis* of the highest order.

Two or three faculty members were chosen to write a critical response to each of the chapters in this book. In this way the seminar became a project of the whole faculty. With regrets we have deemed it infeasible to print the responses; they number over twenty and in some cases are longer than the main essay. Nor is it possible for me to write a summary of the seminar discussions, to reflect the sharpness of the debate, the intricate exchanges, and the spectrum of viewpoints. Certainly nothing resembling a consensus emerged out of our discussions. Nevertheless the experience did teach us where the issues lie and how difficult it is to set limits to the plurality of options that seem to cluster around each of the topics. Instead of attempting a report as such, in the Introduction I will highlight some of the recurrent themes of theological significance, and I will offer some personal comments along the way.

CONTRIBUTORS

Lutheran School of Theology at Chicago

Robert W. Bertram
  Christ Seminary-Seminex Professor of Historical and Systematic Theology

Karen Bloomquist
  Visiting Lecturer in Church and Society and Director of Studies of the Commission for Church and Society, Evangelical Lutheran Church in America

Carl E. Braaten
  Professor of Systematic Theology

Wesley J. Fuerst
  Professor of Old Testament

Edgar M. Krentz
  Christ Seminary-Seminex Professor of New Testament

Jay C. Rochelle
  Associate Professor of Worship, Dean of the Chapel

James A. Scherer
  Professor of Missions and Church History

Franklin Sherman
  Professor of Christian Ethics, Director of Graduate Studies

1

Carl E. Braaten

INTRODUCTION: NAMING THE NAME

W hat is all the fuss about in the naming of God today? As Americans, most of us are born nominalists. We tend to think of names as mere labels. Shakespeare expressed it well when he said a rose by any other name smells as sweet. A name is an empty sound, quite an arbitrary convention. We may choose any number of new metaphors, epithets, and appellations for God and substitute them for the traditional names of God. Names do not really matter that much; we can exchange one set of labels for another, and the underlying reality remains the same. Anyway, mystics tell us that God is the absolutely unknowable One, beyond all names, beyond all naming, something like the Kantian *Ding an sich* that in reality eludes all our predications. We are caught in the prison of our own language; we are born and raised nominalists. It makes it difficult to imagine that our language counts for much of anything when it comes to speaking of God. This is an issue that surfaced again and again in our discussions. At times we were made aware that our nominalistic view of names as labels runs absolutely counter to the mystery of names embodied in the history of religions, including the biblical perspective.

In ancient times the powers of the gods were believed to be present in their names. Calling on the name of one's god in prayer was to invoke its power. The Bible reflects this attitude from beginning to end. The Second Commandment reads: "You shall not take the name of the Lord your God in vain; for the Lord will not hold him guiltless who takes his name in vain" (Exod. 20:7). The Old Testament generally views the name as somehow mystically united with the innermost essence of personal being, divine or human. People will fight to the death to defend their

1

good name or the name of their god. The reality of the divine power seems bound up with the sacred mystery of the name. For the Jews, the divine name Jahweh was too sacred to utter. Jahweh was the proper name of God, and that name was God's personal self-disclosure, and somehow at the same time too holy and dangerous to pronounce.

What a contrast to the present-day mind-set. The Jews believed that God gave himself a name; he revealed himself in his name; it was to be kept holy. Today, we seem to think we can project onto God any name we feel to be a true extension of our self-understanding, thus wittingly or unwittingly confirming Ludwig Feuerbach's projection theory of religion. There can hardly be anything holy about a name that we manipulate in the interest of acquiring a greater self -esteem, however legitimate such an interest might be in purely psychological terms.

The fight for the proper name of God does not end with the Old Testament. The New Testament essayist in this volume, Edgar Krentz, makes the point that there is no proper name of God in the New Testament. The Jewish name of God, Jahweh, is no longer mentioned. A break in the tradition occurred. Nevertheless a new name arises on the soil of the gospel, and that is the name of Jesus, the name above all names (Phil. 2:9), which in due course of time led to a new naming of God as the Holy Trinity: Father, Son, and Holy Spirit. How shall we understand this transition from the radical monotheism of the Hebrew faith to the equally radical christocentric trinitarianism of classical orthodox Christianity? This was one of the recurring themes of our conversations, and the tensions that generally prevail in contemporary theology were clearly in evidence throughout. Neither the Old Testament nor the New Testament chapter on God offers any clue as to how or why the early church found it necessary to complicate its language about God by including the Son and the Holy Spirit on the same doxological plane as its praise of God the Father.

Real Trinitarianism

Speaking of God today takes place in three different contexts—the ecclesial, the academic, and the secular. Within the ecclesial context we speak to God in the language of prayer and praise, and our preaching and teaching can afford to draw upon the kerygmatic-narrative and catechetical-didactic traditions familiar to the Christian family. Within the academic context, God-talk becomes strained and stretched by philosophical questions and metaphysical concepts; theologians have to deal with theories of verification and meaning. In the modern age, theology has kept busy fending off the atheistic criticisms of religion advanced by Feuerbach, Marx, Nietzsche, and Freud. In the 1960s some theologians called themselves Christian atheists, and today, in the 1980s, the deconstructionists are presenting a revised version of atheism (a-theology). The third context in which we speak God's name is the secular realm: the social, political, and economic spheres of activity. In this area, ideologies from the left or the right compete for the church's loyalty, each professing to be on God's side. How can the church speak prophetically God's law and judgment without being taken in by the highest bidder?

It is necessary to have a sophisticated knowledge of the history of theology and of present-day currents of thought to know how to play by the rules of the game appropriate to each of these three contexts of God-language. Many of our difficulties in understanding one another come from the fact that we are mixing these spheres, without being clear that each calls for a different sort of integrity. A fully developed theology must learn to address each of these three publics in an intelligible way without surrendering the principle of identity that makes theology most deeply Christian.

The confusion of the three language spheres to which we have referred becomes clearly manifest in trying to make sense of the doctrine of the Trinity. Not infrequently a colleague will offer the remark: "The Trinity does not make sense to people anymore." What on earth can this mean? It may mean that there is no current philosophical system of concepts that can help explicate trinitarian language. Or it may mean that there is no overwhelming historical-exegetical support for the dogma of the Trinity. Or perhaps it may mean that the Trinity is not existentially relevant, that people of today do not ask the kind of question to which the doctrine responds. What we are witnessing in the case of such comments is a confusion of linguistic contexts. For example, it would be inappropriate to construct a theory of the perichoretic relations between the three members of the Trinity in a forum assembled to debate something like the decline of religion or the meaning of God in a secular age.

In a seminary context, however, one might expect that all minds would share the same ecclesial ground. We read the same Scriptures, subscribe the same confessions, and belong to the same church. Yet, there is far from a real consensus on the logic of trinitarian discourse or the rationale of trinitarian dialectics. Our provincial nominalism tends to shine through at this point as well. This is manifest in the tendency to think that the oneness of God has higher ontological validity than God's threeness. It is sometimes implied that Christians are basically radical monotheists, somewhat like Jews and Muslims, only we have inherited a tradition of symbolizing the one divine Subject in three ways or modes of self-expression. The ancient church dubbed this manner of thinking "Sabellianism." This has been the prevailing explanation of the Trinity since Friedrich Schleiermacher and is still much alive in contemporary Protestant theology. Most theologians seem to be pre-trinitarian theists, starting with the one God and proceeding to the three persons. This has been the dominant line of thinking characteristic of the West, going back perhaps even to Augustine. Today some theologians are asking whether this approach leads to a real Trinity or only to a nominal Trinity.

Karl Rahner and Karl Barth provided a new impetus to trinitarian theology. Rahner postulated a rule that has become virtually axiomatic in new thinking about the Trinity, according to which the immanent Trinity of God's pretemporal eternity is identical with the economic Trinity disclosed in the history of salvation. If this rule is binding on theological thought, it means that the incarnation of the Son of God as a historical event is constitutive of the identity of the eternal God as such. The eternal identity of God cannot be thought apart from the historical events of Jesus' birth and death. Eberhard Jüngel is one who has followed Rahner's rule to its final consequence in asserting the historicity of the eternal God in the perishability of the crucified Jesus. In addition to Jüngel the most significant new trinitarians who are rethinking God on the basis of God's self-revelation in history are Wolfhart Pannenberg, Jürgen Moltmann, Robert W. Jenson, and Walter Kasper. These theologians are not searching for a God above and beyond the events of time and space but locating the coming of God in the history of God's self-identification with the suffering, death, and resurrection of Jesus of Nazareth. Our conversations regrettably never measured up to the challenge of this new thinking on the Trinity.

Luther's Shadow

It should not be surprising that Luther's theology would cast a long shadow over our discussions about God-language. His whole theology was an exercise in fidelity to the Word of God. He was a preacher of the Word and a biblical expositor of the Word; his hermeneutical principle was Word-centered. How was it possible for Luther to have such confidence in the knowability and speakability of the mind and will of God?

Luther knew the *via negativa* which swept all language about God into a nebulous cloud of unknowing. Yet he was bold to speak about the infinite God who had made himself a finite object in the world of human experience. The christological maxim, *finitum capax infiniti* ("the finite is capable of the infinite"), runs counter to the mystical way of canceling the finite step by step in order to ascend to the absolute otherness of God. The mystical way seems so appropriate to the majesty and glory of God; it seems to be the only way to honor the sovereign Deity and carry on the fight against idolatry, which substitutes a finite object for the Wholly Other. For mysticism, silence and emptying our heads of all concrete images of God are the most appropriate ways to acknowledge the presence of the Holy.

Luther would have none of that. He learned from Scripture that the religious attempt to elevate ourselves to the level of God was the root of idolatry; it means that we want to be in control of our encounter with God—on our terms. Furthermore, the other side of idolatry is blasphemy, and that means to scoff or hold in contempt the humble and lowly places where God has elected to meet human beings and to call them into the fellowship of his down-to-earth love. In speaking of God it is so easy to veer from one side to the other, from idolatry to blasphemy, all in the interest of protecting the solemnity of our loftiest mystical or metaphysical notions of God and the piety we have shaped to match them. When Sallie McFague writes, "When we try to speak of God there is nothing which resembles what we can conceive when we say that word,"[1] we have to ask in the spirit of Luther, "Then what on earth is the incarnation for? Then what was Jesus all about?" In a heated moment, one of our colleagues blurted out, "But you don't believe Jesus is God, do you?" I would have thought that the great christological tradition teaches us that the person of Jesus is God incarnate and, as Luther said, "There is no other God."

We can observe two diametrically opposed trends in speaking of God. The one calls itself theocentric, deeply suspicious of anthropomorphic or homocentric models of God-language. Then the links between God and the history of humanity, particularly God's self-embodiment in Jesus of Nazareth, are broken—all of this presumably in fidelity to the theme of *sola Deo gloria*. The other trend is christocentric, which holds that Jesus as subject gives to God as predicate its definitive content and meaning. This is the approach of Luther's theology of the cross. Today we could appropriate the very words of Luther to describe our own

situation: "The theology of the cross has been abrogated, and everything
has been completely turned upside down. . . . A theologian of glory does
not recognize, along with the apostle, the crucified and hidden God
alone."[2] The theology of glory searches for God among the most glorious things in the highest heaven; the theology of the cross meets God
in the suffering and death of the crucified Jew. Luther said: "Some
through their speculations ascend into heaven and speculate about God
the creator, etc. Do not get mixed up with this God. Whoever wishes to
be saved should leave the majestic God alone—for He and the human
creature are enemies."[3] Where, then, can God be found and how can we
speak of him? Luther answered: "[God] does not allow us to find Him in
our thoughts. If we could do this, we would not need God; but because
we need Him, He has designated a place and a person—showing us
where and in what way He ought to be found."[4]

If we follow Luther's cruciform theology, we will be suspicious of the
motives behind the prohibitions of anthropomorphic language about
God, as though such were necessarily demeaning of the true mystery of
the divine. Our suspicion is nurtured by the revolution of the gospel,
which turns our thoughts and language literally upside down, which proclaims the God whose being and life cannot be seen apart from the life,
death, and resurrection of Jesus of Nazareth. When we forget or ignore
this christological basis and content of God-language, we talk a different
language, however reverent our best intentions. And we may not even
notice the change of language, since we are surrounded by a host of sophisticated mystical, metaphysical, psychological, or sociological models
of God-talk that help us to erase from our memories the association of
God with the one in whom there was no "form or comeliness" (Isa. 53:
2).

The Feminist Catalyst

No matter what the topic, the feminist critique of patriarchal and androcentric metaphors of God served our conversations as an ever-pres-
ent catalyst to reopen the question of how to speak most meaningfully of
God today. No one, of course, is going to waste a lot of breath defending
the remnants of a dying patriarchal system. It is not feminist ideology, after all, that has doomed patriarchy; rather, the dominant sociohistorical
forces of the modern world—industrialization, urbanization, socializa-
tion, globalization, scientific and technological institutionalization, and
the like—all these have combined to topple the pillars on which patriar-

chy rests. Man-woman relationships will never be the same again; it is impossible and undesirable to turn back the clock.

One thing is clear. Church women are no longer willing to accept the notion that their place is *Kinder, Küche,* and *Kirche.* Among Protestants there have been strong support and sympathy for the ordination of women, although there is a time lag when it comes to incorporating women into all levels of church leadership. For example, there is not one woman bishop in American Lutheranism, and I know of only a few in the other denominations. We can point to similar discrepancies between the church's inclusivist policy and its practice. I believe that the feminist ideological agenda to get rid of the symbols of God as Father and of Jesus as Son, and to substitute alternative metaphors for the triune name, derives much of its emotional support from people who affirm the legitimate concern of women to be treated as equals in the name of fairness and justice. When feminists examine the place of women in the churches, especially in the Roman Catholic Church, there is a lot of evidence that warrants their charge of sexism. The matter becomes particularly ambiguous at a time when Lutherans, for many good reasons, are working hard to restore their church relations with Orthodox and Catholic communions, the very traditions that are totally opposed to the ordination of women. Some feminists are voicing their suspicion that the Lutheran tilt to the Catholic side of the ecumenical spectrum is a conspiracy to rescind the ordination of women, for seemingly noble ecumenical reasons. And the same suspicion is raised against the voice of Lutherans, including my own, to restore the historic episcopate. If it is historic enough, would it not exclude women? I do not believe, however, that there are real grounds for these suspicions. Nevertheless, the fact that these suspicions exist indicates that we are living in a highly charged politicized atmosphere, in which a conservative attitude toward tampering with our biblically grounded naming of God as Father, Son, and Holy Spirit is easily suspected of being a mask for "keeping women in their place."

There is no consensus among feminists on how to handle God-language. The more conservative wing of feminist theology would go back to the Bible and the Christian tradition and look for feminine metaphors of God, lift them up and balance them with the male metaphors. The more radical wing goes behind the biblical Christian tradition to the cult of Baal in order to restore the goddesses that were vanquished by Jahweh, the male deity. This approach is bent on producing a new religious synthesis, perhaps a new religion or a new church. A third approach is intermediate, which calls for a resymbolization of God from the perspective of women's experience, yet guided by an essential core of truth in the tradition. This approach is different from the first in that new symbols are being constructed and new language is being coined based on contemporary experience. Karen Bloomquist's chapter in this volume on "The Theological Necessity of Depatriarchalizing God" brings out a wealth of feminist perspectives, which show how volatile the topic of God-referring language is at the present time.

The greatest divide in feminist perspectives on God-language occurs in the field of Christology. Christology rests on the assertion that Jesus is the Christ. Some feminists emphasize more the *Jesus* side, others more the *Christ* side. Jesus' maleness is, for some feminists, an insuperable disadvantage. The advantage of the symbol of Christ is that it is neither male nor female but may be interpreted as an empty vessel in which we—from whatever ideological perspective—may pour our own soteriological content. On the other hand, the advantage with Jesus is that he was a concrete historical figure who actually put into practice a new relationship among human beings, emphasizing filiation, love, intimacy, mercy, and friendship, whereas Christ may be an abstract symbol with no concrete liberating historical content. On the crucial issue of Christology the traditional oppositions between ebionites and docetists, adoptionists and incarnationists, and low and high Christology play themselves out on feminist soil as much as they are reflected in the history of the Christian tradition.

New Naming of God

Our studies have shown that there is an ongoing history of naming God in new ways. The greatest challenge today comes not from within the church and the various ideologies circulating within the West but from the front lines of encounter between Christianity and the living world religions. We remember what Peter said, filled with the Holy Spirit: "There is salvation in no one else, for there is no other name under heaven given among men by which we must be saved" (Acts 4:12). We also know that fifth columnists are at work within the church to relativize the exclusivity of Peter's statement, harking back to the liberal Protestant notion that there are many roads that lead to God, many ways of salvation, many savior figures, many paths that lead to the top of Mt. Fuji. As John Hick says, "God has many names." Of course, God has many names, but what is the relation between these many names and the one name that is above all names? We cannot escape the New Testament affirmation that salvation is in the name of Jesus and in no other name. Here the "name" is not a nominalistic label but a symbol of the reality in which it participates (Paul Tillich). The only salvation we have is through participation in the reality symbolized by the name. The Word and the Sacraments are epiphanies of the reality so named.

In the New Testament itself the missionary proclamation named the name and interpreted it by means of many other names. So Jesus was called the Messiah, the Lord, the Son of God, the prophet, the suffering servant of God, the High Priest, the Son of Man, the Savior, the Logos, and numerous other titles. No one of the early Christian communities applied all these titles to identify the person and meaning of Jesus. The choice of the title depended on what each local community had to offer as a term of soteriological significance. The same thing is true around the world today. The moment we step outside the Jewish world of the first apostles, we begin to hear new names applied to Jesus. Jesus' question addressed to Peter on the road to Caesarea Philippi, "Who do you say that I am?" continues to be asked in new missionary settings, evoking new christological responses. When new people hear the gospel of God concerning Jesus and translate that message into their own non-Semitic world of thought, they necessarily convert to new ways of naming God. A positive symbiosis of the original gospel and the thought world of another religion develops, giving expression to the apostolic conviction that the particular name of Jesus has universal implications for the experience of God in all cultures. Who and what God is takes on new dimensions of meaning when all religious rites and performances are done in the name of Jesus, for "at the name of Jesus every knee should bow, in heaven and on earth and under the earth, and every tongue confess that Jesus Christ is Lord, to the glory of God the Father" (Phil. 2:10-11).

James Scherer addresses this issue of new naming of God in his chapter "Missiological Naming," setting that in contrast to "doxological naming" which tends to confine itself to the sacred traditions at home in the Christian family. A certain tension is bound to emerge between the old familiar ways of naming God and the new ways of cross-cultural contextualization mandated by a universal gospel. Learning new ways to name God is always risky but essential to a living global faith that claims to be founded on an event that combines the concrete particularity of Jesus and the universality of divine salvation in his name.

We have covered some of the major areas in which our studies and conversations about God-language unfolded. There are no conclusive results. We are involved in a major task of revisioning our traditions of God-language. We are called to represent the Word of God to the world, and language is our only medium. What we say about God and how we say it matters infinitely to ourselves and others. There are sharp theological differences among us, but these are relativized by a faith whose alpha and omega provide the brackets within which we live and work together.

2

Carl E. Braaten

THE PROBLEM OF GOD-LANGUAGE TODAY

*T*his chapter will dig around in the soil and examine the roots of the problem of God-language today. Just a little bit of digging shows us that the language problem cannot be solved simply by changing metaphors or pronouns for God. A too radical adjustment of religious language may require new roots, perhaps something like what Naomi Goldenberg calls a "changing of the Gods."[1] Changing the language may have the effect of changing the God to whom the language refers. Language is the medium of the divine-human encounter.

The Problem as Old as Creation

As long as we confine the problem of language to an academic debate, we are accustomed to a high toleration of all sorts of verbal experiments in speaking about God. But the native soil of God-language is not primarily that of the academic world inquiring into ways of speaking *about* God—a *descriptive* monological approach. Rather, the native soil is an originally dialogical one, that of prophecy or proclamation, speaking *for* God, which is a *prescriptive* task, as well as that of prayer and praise, speaking *to* God, which is an *ascriptive* act.[2]

After living in the academic world long enough, we may succumb to the illusion of thinking that our artificial ways of speaking *about* God should dictate all the other ways of speaking *for* God and *to* God. We may even wonder why the troops in the field pay so little attention to signals coming from theological headquarters. Theology, however, is a second-order type of reflection. As theologians, we do not cook up God-language and then deliver it like hot cakes to our communities for their consumption. Actually, it is more the other way around. Theology begins its thinking *about* God with the raw materials coming from the traditions of communities that live in the dialogical situation of worship, a kind of conversation going back and forth between the living God and the hearers of God's Word. When theology becomes a world unto itself, it ends up in a scholasticism which Melanchthon attacked as a lot of religious chitchat that talks its subject to death, not respecting the mystery of God.[3]

It is our intention to engage in thinking *about* God within the context and for the sake of the community of faith that continues somehow to speak *for* God to the world and to address God in words of prayer, praise, and thanksgiving. Today we are actually aware that when we set out to think about God, we do not have any clear and distinct idea in our mind. "God is an oblong blur," said John Updike. We are not even sure about how to begin asking the right question. Who is God? What is God? Where is God? Is God a substance? A Being? A Person? A Process? A Verb? Is God near or far? Transcendent or immanent? Within or beyond time? Timeless or everlasting duration? Is God one or three or more in number? Is God's relation to the world to be thought of pantheistically, deistically, or panentheistically? Does God even exist at all? No less a solemn assembly than the Lutheran World Federation in Finland in 1963 issued a message with these words:

> Man today no longer asks: How shall I find a gracious God? His question is much more radical and fundamental. He asks: God, where are you? He does not suffer from the wrath of God, but from a sense of his absence, not from his sin but from the meaninglessness of life. He does not ask for a gracious God, but he asks whether God really exists.

But then Paul Tillich instructs us that, if God is God, it is not appropriate to predicate existence of God as it is of other objects. Wolfhart Pannenberg has caused bafflement by his enigmatic statement, "God does not yet exist." Paul van Buren went one step farther, when he announced: "Today, we cannot even understand the Nietzschean cry that 'God is dead!' for if it were so, how could we know? No, the problem now is that the *word* 'God' is dead."[4]

Are these examples of contemporary theological chitchat? Yet it is not only people of today who are making strange statements about God, wondering about God's absence or silence or about what God is doing or saying, if anything at all. People have a tendency to imagine that the problems they face are unique, unprecedented, and more critical than those of any other time. Isn't it true, however, that in biblical times people were aware of similar difficulties in talking about God? Deutero-Isaiah asks: "To whom then will you liken God, or what likeness compare with him?" (Isa. 40:18). Psalm 10:1 asks, "Why dost thou stand afar off, O Lord? Why dost thou hide thyself in times of trouble?" And Jesus cried the verse in Ps. 22:1: "My God, my God, why hast thou forsaken me?" The Bible does not picture a God easy to believe and simple to define.

Our modern problems may be special in some sense but not necessarily the most profound. As soon as the first philosophers searched for the *logos,* the meaning, of their native rituals and myths, they reflected on the problem of speaking of God in human terms. If we take our language about God as literally descriptive, we run into verbal idolatry. If we retreat to the other side and negate the adequacy of language altogether to speak of God, we run the risk of saying nothing at all. If God is GOD, the utterly transcendent One, how can we human beings speak of God at all? If God, as Karl Barth said, is *totaliter aliter,* then how is real knowledge of God possible? We are caught in the classic catch-22 of the *via negationis.* Fear of idolatry drives monotheists into deep mystical silence. As Bishop John A. T. Robinson put it: "As for the image of God, whether metal or mental, I am prepared to be an agnostic with the agnostic, even an atheist with the atheists."[5] Western theology inherited a Neoplatonist version of the biblical injunction, "You shall not make for yourself a graven image" (Exod. 20:4). The fear is not only of material objects representing God but of mental concepts applied to an infinite inexpressible One. Plotinus said of this One, "It can neither be spoken of nor written of." In fact, he said, "if we are led to think positively of the One, there would be more truth in silence." Yet, Plotinus was a God-intoxicated soul who went on to say many things about this inexpressible One. He saw the problem, as he stated: "It is impossible to say 'not that' if one is utterly without experience or conception of 'that.' "[6] If all human language must be negated for fear of idolatry, then what are we really saying when we not only speak *about* God but also *for* God and *to* God? Tillich acknowledged the problem: "There would be no negation if there were no preceding affirmation to be negated."[7]

The Middle Ages was much preoccupied with the sense of God-language. Duns Scotus, for example, argued for univocal language as applied to God. If God is wholly other than our linguistic concepts and terms, we can have no certain knowledge of God. Thomas Aquinas rejected Scotus's argument, maintaining instead that all knowledge of God is by way of analogy. We have no concepts that can apply univocally both to God and to creatures, because the infinite essence of God renders all our language equivocal. Thomas's analogy principle fell on hard times, first at the hands of the nominalists and later with the rise of critical philosophy stemming from David Hume and Immanuel Kant.

We have lifted out a few names from the tradition to illustrate that the awareness of the problem of God-language seems to be as old as creation. It is not a modern problem, though the debate now goes on in a world situation characterized by institutionalized and ideologized forms of atheism. Theology seems to be nervously oscillating between a total skepticism on the one hand, negating all its concepts for the sake of the divinity of God, at times plunging into hypotheses of despair, from the "death of God" to "secularization" to "deconstructionism," and on the other hand a complete dogmatism which freezes its traditional language to an absolute degree, guaranteed by either the Bible or the pope or the church or the charismatic experience of the Holy Spirit. Luther, in a not altogether dissimilar situation, was aware that our God-language was the language of faith and confession (*Gott and Glaube gehören zuhaufe!*), knowing full well that "the language of symbols is the mother tongue of faith"[8] (Gustaf Aulén). Yet he countered Erasmus's skepticism with the words, "Take away assertions, and you take away Christianity (*Tolle assertiones, et Christianissimum tulisti*).[9] In our century, Tillich coined the expression "belief-ful realism" to describe a position that was perhaps substantially the same. The knowledge of faith is real knowledge of God that comes to expression in forms of language that refer to events and interpretations that faith sees as originating in God's revelation and that it claims as its basis and contents. When faith speaks of God, it does not have in mind any god whatsoever; it is very particular about the identity of the God *for* whom and *to* whom it speaks. Faith has no passion to breathe new life into the dying gods of this age. The announcement that "God is dead" may be good news after all, depending on the identity of the god in question.

The Deconstruction of Theism

Sallie McFague opens her book *Metaphorical Theology* with the words from Simone Weil's mystical book *Waiting for God:* "There is a God. There is no God. Where is the problem? I am quite sure that there is a God in the sense that I am sure my love is no illusion. I am quite sure there is no God in the sense that I am sure there is nothing which resembles what I can conceive when I say that word."[10] Then, after exploring the potential of language to speak of God, particularly parabolic and metaphorical language, McFague concludes where she began: "The last word as well as the first word in theology is surrounded by silence. We know with Simone Weil that when we try to speak of God there is nothing which resembles what we can conceive when we say that word."[11] What are we to make of this mystical confession if it should perchance claim to be a piece of Christian theological reflection, whose alpha and omega is not silence (sigé was in fact a gnostic aeon) but the Word of God who breaks the silence, who is and who was and who is to come?[12] If someone should bring the news that the god enshrouded in silence is dead, having had to yield to the living God who speaks really and truly through the Word, the first and the last Word, and who is therefore also the beginning and the end of theos-logos, then it may very well be that we should receive such news with amens and hallelujahs. It all depends on which God is dead.

The floodgates of atheism are wide open. Never before has Christian theology done its constructive work in the face of atheism to quite the same extent as today. The two most impressive systematic theologians of our day, Eberhard Jüngel and Wolfhart Pannenberg, explicitly think through what they mean by "God" in the face of the challenges and criticisms of atheism. They do it in very different ways, to be sure, but both are intent on discovering the logic of the language of faith. Traditionally, Christian theology could count on the philosophers to help them explain the language and logic of theology. But, in our time, there is no God of the philosophers to speak of. What we have are the "God-equivalents" of Martin Heidegger, Ludwig Wittgenstein, and Alfred North Whitehead, gods which theologians have been trying to milk of every last drop of apologetic value. But where has that gotten us? How has it helped the community of faith to speak for God and to God with a better conscience, and more powerfully and faithfully? Blaise Pascal contrasted the God of the patriarchs with the God of the philosophers. Was he right, after all?

In the last two centuries, theology has had to cope with a series of atheistic accounts of its use of God-language. From Ludwig Feuerbach's theory of God-language as a projection of human longing for infinity, to Karl Marx's theory of God-language as the consolation of the poor serv-

ing the vested interests of the rich, to Sigmund Freud's notion of God as
an infantile illusion, to Friedrich Nietzsche's interpretation of religion as
springing from the *ressentiment* of the masses, we have wave upon wave
washing away the foundations of theistic God-language.[13] Theology has
countered these atheistic theories with various sandbagging fortifica-
tions to repair breaches in its system of Christian truth. Apologetics has
rushed to the defense of belief in God, as though the entire Christian
symbol system depended on it for survival. But, already by this time, the
specifically Christian trinitarian doctrine of God had been relegated to
an appendix of Christian dogmatics, exposing the God of its prolego-
mena to the combined force of the modern atheistic criticisms. But this
God was not the Trinity of Christian faith. It was the now putrefied remains of the God of the philosophers, the God of natural theology, the
unbaptized theism of unitarian metaphysics, which was always intended
to serve as a kind of ramp leading into the heart of Christian dogmatics,
structured by its trinitarian and christological belief system.

The theological tradition, reaching back to the patristic period
through pre- and post-Reformation scholasticism, through Thomas
Aquinas and Augustine, had given God a Dr. Jekyll and Mr. Hyde per-
sonality, splitting the doctrine of God into two parts, separating its discussion *de deo uno* from *de deo trino*, giving rise to a widespread feeling
that the former is prior and fundamental, while the latter is but a late
emergence at a lower level of symbolization, if not actually only a non-
essential theologoumenon easily removed. Adolf von Harnack and Wilhelm Herrmann were to argue that the Trinity was not essential to Luther's faith; it only stuck to it as a piece of eggshell from the old
ecclesiastical synthesis. The two aspects, the unity and the trinity of God,
were thus divided, with the result that the dogmatics and apologetics of
modern theology since Friedrich Schleiermacher inflated the theme of
unity at the expense of trinity, and in such a way that the unitarian formulations about God became increasingly remote from the specifically
Christian trinitarian language of God, even putting them at odds with
each other. The theism of the academic theological establishment eroded
the foundations of trinitarian theology by attempting to speak of God
without Christ, of the Father without the Son, of the Creator apart from
the covenant, isolating the first article of the Creed from the second and
third articles and thereby distorting it.

With the collapse of trinitarian discourse, modern theology yielded
to an abstract metaphysical preoccupation with a bloodless and faceless

being of God. It was this God in its splendid isolation that became the vulnerable target of the atheistic sharpshooters of modern times—Feuerbach, Marx, Freud, Nietzsche, and others. It is not a Christian virtue to rejoice when someone is getting killed, but the announcement of the "death of God" was greeted in some Christian circles with joy and thanksgiving. The irony is that the closer a particular theology stuck to the central place of Christ in the Christian symbol system, the easier it was to bid adieu to the nontrinitarian God-construct of post-Enlightenment theism. Albrecht Ritschl planted the seeds of this inner-theological accommodation of the deconstruction of metaphysical theism, but Barth reaped the harvest with his reconstruction of the Christian doctrine of God in radically christocentric trinitarian terms. The "death of God" theology of the 1960s may be seen as a delayed reaction, on American soil, to the dissolution of theism. Gabriel Vahanian, Paul van Buren, William Hamilton, and Thomas J. J. Altizer were all bellowing out the death of God in a language that betrayed their Barthian accent, but they were unable to preserve the integrity of the language of faith for lack of an adequate conceptual framework provided by the trinitarian formula.

The atheistic challenges to metaphysical theism have, therefore, been met by a variety of responses. We can mention three main types. First, the end of theism may be embraced in the way that Altizer and others who call themselves deconstructionists do. In addition to Altizer—who is the bridge from the "death of God" theology of the 1960s to the deconstructionism of the 1980s—we may mention Mark C. Taylor, Charles Winquist, Carl A. Raschke, and, somehow, Robert P. Scharlemann as well.[14] They are an interesting collection of voices, taking their inspiration from Nietzsche, Heidegger, Derrida, Foucault, Rorty, and others. In Raschke's words: "Deconstruction is the death of God put into writing. . . . But if God dies, so must theology. . . . Theology must write itself into the grave. . . . Deconstruction within theology writes the epitaph for the dead God. . . . Deconstruction is the dance of death upon the tomb of God."[15]

A second response to the demise of theism follows in the wake of Barth's return to specifically Christian roots. Hermeneutical theology is essentially a retrieval operation, taking a more exegetical turn in Rudolf Bultmann and his school and a more dogmatic shape in Barth and his followers. Gerhard Ebeling and Eberhard Jüngel proceeded to combine features of both strategies. The common feature is to begin theology on the inside of the faith experience, where the event of God's self-revela-

tion itself establishes the meaning of God. This movement is characterized by the rejection of foundationalism; that is, the attempt to found
theology on some general anthropological principles. In the United
States, this neo-Barthian line is evident in what is called the new Yale
school of theology, typified by Hans Frei, David Kelsey, Paul Holmer,
George Lindbeck, Ronald Thiemann, and others. As a background theory, they are likely to appeal to Clifford Geertz's theory of "religion as a
cultural system"[16] and to Wittgenstein's theory of religion as a "language-
game" played by its own set of rules.[17]

A third response to the decline of theism is to defend it at all costs.
This is the approach of the Anglo-Saxon mainline where the old tradition
of apologetics has been continued, only curiously without any dogmatics to back it up. This apologetic recuperation of theism usually takes the
form of recruiting some philosophical ally who still has a few impressive
reasons to believe in God. This is why one school of theology latches on
to Heidegger's language about "Being." This is the approach of John Macquarrie, who thinks that Heidegger's ontological talk about the "letting-
be of Being" will renew today's God-language. A second type of apologetic rescue of theism has adopted the theistic metaphysics of Alfred
North Whitehead and Charles Hartshorne. In *The Reality of God*, Schubert Ogden states: "It is my belief that the conceptuality provided by this
new philosophy enables us so to conceive the reality of God that we may
respect all that is legitimate in modern secularity, while also respecting
fully the distinctive claims of Christian faith itself."[18] Those who currently agree with Ogden are many: Daniel Day Williams (deceased),
Norman W. Pittenger, John Cobb, David Griffin, Paul Sponheim, to mention a few of the more published names.

As an apologetic strategy to build a bridge from contemporary culture to Christian faith, the case for the choice of either a Heideggerian or
a Whiteheadian conceptuality is not very persuasive. The consumers of
either type of apologetics happen to be all believers inside the church,
who may have been inveigled into believing that the language of the
Christian faith will become more intelligible and credible to the modern
cultured despisers of religion when translated into the categories of philosophy. For this reason, the leaders of process theology have to work
hard at persuading people to become Whiteheadians so that their apologetic defense of theistic God-language will work. This is like a call for a
new circumcision. The approach of process theology seems to be incap-
able of relating itself to the real cultural situation of today, particularly

among Americans, who have no taste for metaphysics. Moreover, its interpretation of the Christian faith seems to represent only a torso of the real thing.

The Existential Locus of God-Language

Inasmuch as the deconstructionist strategy offers no future for theology, since of its own admission it signals the end of the road, and inasmuch as neither the existential-ontological system of Heidegger nor the process philosophical categories of Whitehead promise to drive Christian theology more deeply into its own themes and symbols of meaning, it would seem that we have painted ourselves into a Barthian corner. Jüngel, who stands for a kind of Barthian renaissance, writes:

> There are two approaches in contemporary theology by which the attempt is being made to learn to think God again. The one way, pursued by Wolfhart Pannenberg with impressive consequentiality, is to think "God having been removed" *(remoto deo)* in order to arrive at the disclosure of the thought of God, which then functions as the framework for the Christian faith's own understanding of God. The studies in this book [Jüngel's *God as the Mystery of the World*] will take the opposite approach. The thinking here pursues a path which, one might say, goes from the inside toward the outside, from the specifically Christian faith experience to a concept of God which claims universal validity. The goal of the intellectual route adopted in this book is not to demonstrate the thinkability of God on the basis of general anthropological definitions, but rather to think God and also man on the basis of God's self-disclosure which leads to the experience of God, and thus to demonstrate that the Christian truth is universally valid on the basis of its inner power.[19]

I think that the Barth-Jüngel line has much to commend it, judged by its fruits. In renouncing the apologetic task, it can concentrate all its creative energies on the interpretation of the language of faith and doctrine for the sake of the church. Since it has no great investment in any one set of pretheological categories, it is free to pick and choose from all kinds of sources. Barth admitted that there were many philosophical noodles in his soup; it's just that he was not committed to any particular brand. Similarly, the antifoundationalism of Lindbeck[20] and others frees them to explore the grammar of the language of faith in its canonical and confessional texts (intratextuality), a repristinating strategy of a conservative heart. Judged by its fruits, it is an approach that works. Lindbeck is perhaps the most significant architect of twentieth-century ecumenical and interconfessional theology we could name. Yet I have deep reservations.

Given the two options cited by Jüngel, I find myself going to the other side. The purely intraecclesial and intratextual dogmatic option of Barth and his new American friends cannot contain the question of God and its answer. The issues of contemporary consciousness press in upon us, and they exceed the limits of the Bible and the church. The problem of God-language is not any longer chiefly a problem arising in the controversy between theism and atheism; it is one that has arisen within the context of the church itself. It is, thus, an issue not only between believers and unbelievers but among believers themselves. Believers as such are worrying about what it means to speak of God today, not only to communicate with people outside the church but to liberate and broaden their language for the sake of the gospel itself, in order that communities of faith may better speak *for* God and *to* God. God-language is, therefore, a matter not only of apologetic concern but also of crucial liturgical import. How shall we as believers in Jesus Christ and members of his church use language of God in the various situations of witness and worship?

For the reasons we have mentioned, we should try to take theological responsibility for the entire waterfront of issues that concern people who already believe (dogmatics) as well as those who do not yet believe (apologetics). Process theologians tend to do apologetics without dogmatics, while the Barthians tend to do dogmatics without apologetics. A pure theology of revelation without grounding itself in anthropology seems to me to stand theology on its head.[21] My esteem for the theological program of Pannenberg and my ongoing indebtedness to Tillich's method of correlation are due to their comprehensive interest in the full range of apologetic and dogmatic sorts of inquiry.

The epistemological priority of the question of God calls for "a new style of natural theology."[22] The question of God is a religious question, one that Christians in some way share with people of all religions, and even of no religion at all. The question of God arises out of the human quest for meaning; it is, thus, a structural dimension of human existence. Statements and symbols about God function to answer questions concerning the nature and destiny of human existence. Through analysis of the human subject, it can be shown that human beings do strive to transcend beyond all the givens of their experience, to discover what lies beyond their limits. Peter Berger aptly refers to these experiential elements in the self-surpassing openness of the human subject as "signals of transcendence."[23] These signals are not like the proofs of the existence of God in the old-style natural theology. This new-style natural theology stops short of claiming to possess definitive knowledge of God and God's will unto salvation, on which the life of faith, hope, and love is founded. But it does ground the meaning of the idea of God in the structures of common human experience. It is starting theology "from below," from the side of the human subject inquiring into the possibilities of meaning in existence and history. It does not begin "from above," from the sheer datum of revelation (cf. Dietrich Bonhoeffer's *Offenbarungspositivismus*). Pannenberg's massive new *Anthropology in Theological Perspective*[24] shows how the various sciences of the human spirit have discovered many dimensions of experience that can be most adequately understood in the light of the religious quest for God. The partial meanings in our experience cry out for a final and total context of meaning.

The priority of anthropology in theological method runs counter to the Barthian interdiction against philosophy, natural theology, and apologetics, but it is mandated, I think, by the Lutheran sense of the priority of law over gospel. The Lutheran sequence of law and gospel is at the base of Tillich's method of correlating the human situation and the divine message. When Tillich characterized Luther's method in terms of the "law of contrasts," he had in mind Luther's distinction between God's two ways of working in the world. I see a linkage between Luther's law/gospel dialectic, Tillich's method of correlation, and Pannenberg's anthropology in theological perspective.

If we follow this trajectory of ideas, we are in a better position to understand the dark negative side of religious experience today, which the deconstructionists are thematizing. Altizer calls this the contemporary experience of "the anonymity of God,"[25] the features of which can hardly fail to recall Luther's description of the experience of the "hidden God" (*Deus absconditus*). The death-of-god deconstructionists are themselves aware of their Luther connection as they play with the words *theologia crucis* and *crux theologiae*.

A new-style natural theology can function as an instrument of theology exploring human experience in the light of the law. We would prefer to call it simply a phenomenology of experience from a theological perspective. In such a phenomenology we can take seriously the language that reveals the ways that human beings experience themselves in the world. This is the experience of the anonymous God, the God who is hiddenly active in the world, the unknown God to whom people of today build altars of money, power, race, sex, nation, and religion on which to offer up human sacrifices. This is the God who is the nameless presence of mystical religious experience, the one enshrined in the silence of Simone Weil and Sallie McFague. This is the God who exerts a pressure behind the backs of all persons and institutions to do what is right, demand justice, apply the law, and secure the common good, even, at times, against their own self-interests. This God meets us under the guise of many masks, the God who shows us his derrière, which Luther warned us not to mistake for his face. This experience of God is so uncertain, undependable, and untrustworthy that we oscillate between faintheartedness and fanaticism, profanity and idolatry, nihilism and mysticism.

Today, many people wonder whether their God-experiences and God-words refer to anything real at all. If not, then they refer to nothing, and nothing is not much to get excited about. Even this minus sign can be seen as a negative signal of transcendence in the throes of the dissonant experience of God under the condition of the law. Luther had a deep insight into this experience, as have the twentieth-century existentialists and deconstructionists. "Who or what [God] is who is rightly called God, [reason] does not know. . . . Therefore, reason plays blind man's bluff with God; it always misses him and strikes wrong by calling God what is not God, and then again by not calling God what is God. . . . It therefore flops so terribly and gives the name and divine honor and calls God what it thinks God is, and never hits upon the right God, but always upon the devil, or its own pride, which is ruled by the devil."[26]

If we look for traces of transcendence and mystery in human experience and language, we will gain some points of contact for the specifically Christian language of God coming from the Bible and the traditions of the church. Theodore Jennings, taking clues from the writings of Ebeling, Kierkegaard, Heidegger, Tillich, Ramsey, Gilkey, Bloch, Moltmann, and others, has composed a list of *existentialia,* locating and identifying the typical generating occasions of God-language from various regions of human experience—ontological, aesthetic, and historical. These are experiential occasions in which a kind of rupturing of our ordinary language takes place, and we say something expletive such as, "Oh, my God!" Here is the list: peace, despair, awe, wonder, joy, terror, dread, hope, abandonment, and love. Jennings calls these the "radical affections," recalling Jonathan Edwards's analysis of the "religious affections."[27] Such a phenomenology can be very helpful, not in any sense of proving God or guaranteeing the referentiality of our God-language but in the sense of reconnecting our language about God with real human experiences. Of course, each item in the list of "radical affections" may be interpreted from other perspectives. All we can claim is that a phenomenology of experience and its associated language makes a good fit with the language of God we have learned to speak from the Bible and the Christian tradition. As Tillich once said in a similar connection: "Existentialism is the good luck of Christian theology."[28] A deeper analysis might even show that Christian theology is the mother of modern existentialism, that the deepest self-knowledge is a reflection of the human situation *coram Deo*.

On the Referentiality of God-Language

It may be suspected that our new-style natural theology is not theology at all. It may be only anthropology, and so we may not have escaped Feuerbach's trap. We may not have crossed over Lessing's "ugly ditch" between the merely historical here and now and the great metaphysical yonder. We may not have provided any answer to the "masters of suspicion." I admit that this is true. The conviction that our language about God is referential in kind, that "God" refers to GOD, is itself a matter of experience, a contingent experience, not a necessary universal predicate of human existence. We can call this experience a "leap of faith" (Kierkegaard), "ultimate concern" (Tillich), "existential commitment" (Bultmann), "basic trust" (Hans Küng), or some such thing. Maybe it is just plain old-fashioned "conversion."

A special problem arises when theology loses interest in the referentiality of its own God-language and imagines that it can get on without such a presupposition embraced by faith. Gilkey put his finger on the problem in *Naming the Whirlwind*: "The reality of God and so of the referent of religious language is the central point at issue."[29] In *Language, Logic and God*, Frederick Ferré writes: "Without the element of *belief in* the reality of a referent designated by theological language, the distinctively religious character of this speech is sought in vain."[30] Theism has preoccupied itself with evidences for belief in God and has come up with a revised version of the God of the philosophers. The issue of referentiality is important to contemporary theists. I doubt that real theology of any kind can be done without it. But that alone does not answer the question, "What God are you talking about?" Our bone of contention with traditional unitarian theism was that it is not explicitly the God and Father of Jesus Christ.

There is currently under way a movement beyond theism that boldly surrenders the principle of referentiality. Sharon Welch, in *Communities of Resistence and Solidarity,* has projected a "feminist theology of liberation." She begins her book with a chapter on "the fundamental crisis in Christian theology." The problem, she writes, "concerns the reality referent of Christian faith and thus of Christian theology."[31] "Paul, Aquinas, Luther, and Tillich all assume that faith refers to something real, an experience of ultimacy that is in some way actual and present, an ultimacy that limits and shapes the nature of theological inquiry. We modern academic theologians no longer have the surety of such a referent."[32] Her critique of Latin American liberation theology lies in its never-questioned assumption about the reality of God and the truth reference of its language. In Welch's theology of liberation the referent is not *God* but *liberating,* not the noun but the verb. "That is, the language here is true not because it corresponds with something in the divine nature but because it leads to actual liberation in history."[33]

In the same vein, Sheila Davaney, in an unpublished paper, "Radical Historicity and the Search for Sure Foundations," discusses reformist (Rosemary Radford Ruether and Elisabeth Schüssler Fiorenza) and revolutionary (Mary Daly) proposals for feminist theology. She finds that the two wings of feminist theology are united in their commitment to the ontological reality of God and that, underlying all the oppressive patriarchal distortions of religion, there is a normative source and ground of human values to which theology can appeal. Following Gordon Kaufman's theory of God-language as the imaginative construction of the human mind, as well as Richard Rorty's rejection of the classical correspondence theory of truth, which assumes that the task of thought is to mirror reality in some fashion,[34] Sheila Davaney calls upon feminist theology to give up "the appeal to ontological reality as a grounds of validation for our positions."[35] Where does this land theology? In the blind alley of radical relativism, according to which our "religious symbols would be interpreted . . . as solely the products of human imagination and the projections of human values and desires."[36] The ghost of Feuerbach, no longer hiding in the background, has taken charge of the entire theological operation.

Surrender of the referential meaning of God-language has occurred also on another front, stemming not from continental atheism but instead from Anglo-Saxon empiricism, championed first by David Hume. Hume said there are only two kinds of meaningful statements, those purely definitional and tautological and those reporting matters of fact about the world. Since any theological text that one picks up, including the Bible, contains many other sorts of statements, Hume's counsel was, "Commit it to the flames: for it contains nothing but sophistry and illusion."[37] A. J. Ayer renewed Hume's attack on theology in his famous manifesto, *Language, Truth and Logic.* He laid down the hard-line verification principle of meaning. For a statement to be meaningful, it must be empirically verifiable. This obviously rules out all God-talk, relegating it to the category of pure nonsense. Wittgenstein's *Tractatus* was not so dogmatic. He allowed that "there are, indeed, things that cannot be put into words . . . . They are what is mystical."[38] He ended his book with this oft-quoted statement: "What we cannot speak about we must consign to silence."[39] And since "God does not reveal himself *in* the world,"[40] we must be silent about things mystical.

The problem with Ayer's theory of meaning became quickly apparent: his principle of verification would be meaningless on its own grounds, for it is neither tautological nor empirically verifiable. Yet the effect of the Wittgenstein-Ayer theory of language has been reductionistic and iconoclastic. Paul van Buren's application of the empiricist canon led to semantical atheism, leaving us with a world in the hands of Jesus but without God, for "we do not know 'what' God is, and we cannot understand how the word 'God' is being used."[41]

Van Buren's a-theology was a *reductio ad absurdum,* which he has since recanted. More promising was a new opening provided by the publication of the later Wittgenstein's *Philosophical Investigations.* Theologians found a reprieve in Wittgenstein's theory of "language-games." An analysis of our ordinary language shows that, in fact, a great deal of our language is meaningful without being reducible to statements tautological (2 plus 2 equals 4) or empirical (the hat is on my head). Wittgenstein's new proposal was that we should discover the meaning of language from the way it actually is used in ordinary language. Language usage determines meaning. Theologians such as I. M. Ramsey in *Religious Language* discovered a particular logic and structure in the regular language of faith and worship; it is the task of theology to learn and teach the rules of the language. Theology is the grammar of the language of faith.

A heavy burden seemed to have been removed from the shoulders of theology. For the last decades some theologians have followed Ramsey, particularly in Britain, studying the rules and writing grammar books for a language that fewer and fewer people are speaking and understanding. The problem is that this theology of ordinary language has not exorcized the demon of positivism. It has not allayed the suspicion that perhaps the religious language game lacks reference to anything beyond itself or *us*, that, indeed, it may not be true. A purely functionalist analysis of the language of Christian faith in all its odd varieties does nothing to address the issue of referentiality and truth claim. Learning the way a language works does not legitimate its right to claim our ultimate loyalty. We must be assured that it conveys the truth about ultimate reality.

The Feminist Critique of "God the Father"

Mary Daly has beckoned theology to think its way "beyond God the Father," the title of her truly epoch-making book. It is epoch-making in that all feminist theology abuts up against it and seems forced to measure itself by its standard. Daly has asked theology to enter into the abysmal depths of Tillich's ground of being itself, which is a kind of Schellingian "night in which all cows are black." Who is this Father-God against which Mary Daly protests for the sake of women's freedom and dignity? This is the patriarchal Father who presides over the status quo, which legitimizes and sacralizes the domination of men over women. He is the absolutely transcendent, almighty, and self-sufficient ruler of the universe, whose authority is reduplicated in the hierarchical structures of society, men on top and women on the bottom. This is why women have been prevented from finding full meaning for themselves personally, physically, and sexually.

Mary Daly is describing the traditional patriarchal model of God in a world shaped like a pyramid. At the bottom is the family unit, with the *paterfamilias* owning his wives and children and servants and cattle. At the next level is the fatherland, governed by the *paterpatriae*, who rules over the nation like a father over his family. On the next plane are the religious authorities, who, in the patriarchal system, are called the church fathers, and at the top of this hierarchy is the Holy Father. The whole system has determined that women would be impotent, subject and inferior, proscribing them from any official or sacramental responsibility in the church or the liturgy.

The attack on the image of "God the Father" is directed against the pyramidal hierarchical system over which this Lord-God presides. The feminist polemic against "God the Father" has made some people in the church and some theologians angry and defensive. But as long as the patriarchal system prevails the protest will continue, and we should certainly be a part of it. This Father-God, as far as I can recognize him, is not the God and Father of Jesus Christ. The image of "God the Father" is ambiguous; it has a double background, the one being the patriarchal system and the other the revolutionary Jesus tradition.

The patriarchal Father-God has become the reigning figure in Jewish, Muslim, and Christian monotheism. Jewish-Christian monotheism allied itself with Hellenistic philosophical monism as well as the political monarchism of imperial Rome. This means that the religion, philosophy, and politics of the time produced a massive patriarchal synthesis in which the image of God as Almighty Father expressed itself. When the first article of the Creed separated itself from the second and third—first as an apologetic move within Christian theology, then as an apostate move of the Enlightenment philosophers against Christianity in the name of natural religion—we had the background for the unitarian theism which increasingly isolated itself from the God of the gospel of Jesus Christ. Large sections of modern Christianity are still stuck in that synthesis, and, because of this, many people find themselves driven from the church of "God the Father" or attracted to the altars of the Great Earth Mother as a symbol of life and liberation.

Abusus non tollit usum. God the Father of Jesus Christ is not synonymous with the God of the patriarchal system, religious monotheism, philosophical monism, or political monarchism, or of the Christendom that amalgamated them all into the religion of the Holy Roman Empire. This is the precise target of Luther's verdict when he says that it "strikes wrong by calling God what is not God, and then again by not calling God what is God. . . . [It] calls God what it thinks God is, and never hits upon the right God, but always upon the devil."[42] When the radical feminists such as Mary Daly describe God the Father and his attributes, we see a close family resemblance to the devil. Apart from the gospel, it is hard to tell the difference.

Elisabeth Schüssler Fiorenza, as critical as Mary Daly of the God of the patriarchal system and the androcentric aspects of biblical religion itself, moves us not to some God beyond God the Father but into the locus of biblical revelation itself, which critically breaks away from patriarchal religion and culture. Such "revelation is found in the life and ministry of Jesus as well as in the discipleship community of equals called forth by him."[43] She writes about "the basileia vision of Jesus as the praxis of inclusive wholeness"[44] and exegetes the texts that support her thesis. "The praxis and vision of Jesus and his movement is best understood as an inner-Jewish renewal movement that presented an *alternate* option to the dominant patriarchal structures rather than an oppositional formation rejecting the values and praxis of Judaism."[45] Rosemary Radford Ruether agrees with what she calls Schüssler Fiorenza's reconstruction of the countercultural egalitarian vision of the Jesus movement but stresses even more its links with the Hebraic prophetic tradition. Sallie McFague agrees with Schüssler Fiorenza and Ruether, holding that the divine-human relationship "modeled in the parables and in Jesus as parable of God is intrinsically destructive of conventional power arrangements and hence liberating to those who are oppressed, whether by their sex, race, economic situation, or other factors."[46]

What, then, are the implications of these views for the fatherhood of God? Robert Hamerton-Kelly, in *God the Father*, has argued that Jesus' address to God as "Abba" includes features that destabilize the traditional patriarchal model, features that may be said to be just as maternal as paternal, such as love and compassion. Mary Daly says, "If God is male, then the male is God."[47] "Father" and "Abba" are male-gender terms. Are they hopelessly tied to the patriarchal system? Can we still use the metaphor of Father for God? As a metaphor, it does not describe God. God is not literally a Father. As Sallie McFague points out in *Metaphorical Theology*, the metaphor of "Father" describes a relationship, so the point is not that God is like a human father but that all human beings are like brothers and sisters. It is about human filiation, about all of *us* in a community of equals, sons and daughters, women and men.[48]

Should we get rid of the symbol of "God the Father" or should we continue to interpret it by the criterion of the gospel? Can we work to free ourselves from all the ways and works of the patriarchal system, in our families, nations, and churches, without sacrificing the Father on the altar of such a liberation movement? If we lop off this symbol, which is the next one to go? What symbol escapes pristine pure from the distorting traditions of religion? Paul Ricoeur states: "The symbol gives rise to thought."[49] I believe our task is not to eliminate the symbol, which is a structural linguistic element of the language of the gospel, but to interpret it within a paradigm that can motivate and sustain movements for personal freedom, social equality, and human solidarity.

Toward a New Trinitarian Paradigm

In contemporary thinking about God, there is a great divide in the face of a common crisis. On the one side are those who respond to the problem of anthropomorphic language of God by opting for some nameless God beyond all concreteness, rapt in mystical silence. Down this road the traffic merges with atheism. On the other side are those who follow the incarnational current deep into history, into the concreteness of human flesh. This is the logic of God incarnate in the person of Jesus—the normative locus of revelation which at least one version of feminist theology shares with the classical Christian tradition. The Christian tradition has unanimously pointed to the event of Jesus the Christ as the answer to the question of where and how God is definitively revealed to the world, communicating benefits of salvation and liberation for all human beings. The Christian faith stands or falls with God's self-revelation in Jesus of Nazareth.

It is at this point that we come upon the root of the doctrine of the Trinity. Something like a new trinitarian paradigm is called for. Such a paradigm functions not only in the elaboration of Christian doctrine for the sake of convenience but also to identify the antecedent conditions of the meaning of Christian language of God. In the technical language of the new trinitarian paradigm, the economic and the immanent Trinity are one and the same. This means that our God-language will reflect the very structure of revelation. If Jesus is the revelation of God's true identity, then Jesus is God in the sense that the subject "Jesus" gives to the predicate "God" its definitive content and meaning.[50] Jesus Immanuel represents God to us—*Deus praesens*. Christian faith is not a radical monotheism, after all, as H. Richard Niebuhr alleged. It is a christocentric trinitarian monotheism. The current retreat to theocentricity—James Gustafson,[51] John Hick,[52] Paul Knitter,[53] Tom Driver[54]—is being advocated at the expense of christocentricity. They balk at the notion of a radical incarnation—the *finitum capax infiniti*. They would prefer to look for God *extra carnem Christi*. They are left with a God without the Word and a Word without the flesh. There are many options in that direction—gnosticism, unitarianism, deism, pantheism.

The task of the reconstruction of the trinitarian dogma is being undertaken today, and I believe that this may help to focus and structure our language about God. Diametrically opposed to the antichristological trend in contemporary theology is a movement to continue the Barthian initiative toward a new affirmation of the Trinity on the basis of Christology. New proposals on the Trinity are being offered by Jüngel,[55] Moltmann,[56] Jenson,[57] and Pannenberg.[58] In Catholic theology, a similar line was inaugurated by Karl Rahner[59] and has been continued by Walter Kasper.[60] All of these represent a significant advance to a new conception of the Trinity. It is a regrettable fact that many theologians look upon the Trinity as a piece of dead speculation, following Harnack's verdict, in his *History of Dogma*, that the Trinity was a product of the Hellenization of Christianity. The new theologies of the Trinity argue that, so far from being a mere "memory aid" to organize various topics of Christian belief (Schleiermacher's approach), the root of the Trinity doctrine lies in biblical soil, in the economy of divine revelation and salvation. The Trinity is an indispensable and integral part of the Christian apprehension of God, not an arbitrary set of symbols intending to say something else more fundamental.

Only a new formulation of the Trinity can make clear the identity and nature of the biblical God, the God of the gospel and of Christian faith. This new formulation calls for the death of some ancient assumptions about God. The God of the great patristic synthesis had to be impassible and immutable. This was an assumption taken over from the metaphysical monotheism of Greek philosophical thought. The God of the gospel, in contrast, is one who suffers. Bonhoeffer put it so succinctly: "Only a suffering God can help."[61]

Process theism has also challenged the patristic idea of the divine metaphysical attributes of impassibility and immutability and calls upon the philosophy of Whitehead to make its case for the primacy of the category of *becoming* in God. However, the approach of process theology has led to a dipolar concept of God and makes its identification of God apart from trinitarian dialectics. This is because, for process theology, the event of Jesus Christ is not constitutive of our knowledge of God but is, at best, only its exemplification. Only after it gets its doctrine of God rolling does process thought, at a later stage, begin to worry about the sense of specifically Christian symbolism, so that Christology and Trinity appear as addenda to a theistic metaphysics. The approach of genuine trinitarian thinkers moves in the opposite direction. Pannenberg has said:

"Wherever philosophical concepts are taken over, they must be re-molded in the light of the history-shaping freedom of the biblical God."[62] Pannenberg has now written a full-scale doctrine of the Trinity in his newly published *Systematische Theologie*, which clearly indicates that he is part of the movement to revise and renew trinitarian theology.[63] I am convinced that this is the right direction to go in dealing with the most pressing theological question of who and what we are prepared to name God.[64]

Why the Trinity, after all? The reason is that the identity of God is not separable from the integrity of God's actions. We do not look for the inner nature of God in some remote sphere above and beyond the structure of God's operations in and upon the world. A theology that begins its doctrine of God with trinitarian dialectics is a way of speaking faithfully of the God of the gospel of Good Friday, Easter, and Pentecost.

The implications of trinitarian revisionism will be far-reaching. The political implictions of trinitarian dialectics can be vastly different from the hierarchical relations presided over by the Sovereign Monad of the various unitarianisms, monisms, and monarchisms. The God of the gospel is not comfortable being assigned a role at the top of the Constantinian pyramid, in which every class has its place and every person his or her task, promoting both an authoritarian and a class-structured society. The new social model of the Trinity is critical of the monotheistic monarchianism that has dominated the traditional concept of the Trinity which undergirds the patriarchal system. The image of the omnipotent male monarch as traditionally derived from the patriarchal religions does not fit the social image of God that we find in the unity of the divine fellowship of personal relations as Father-Son-Spirit. The Father Almighty is then no longer the archetype of the imperial rulers of this world but rather the compassionate Father of the crucified Jesus. The cross represents a reversal of the image of God, wherein the Almighty becomes manifest in powerlessness, suffering, pain and death. Almighty power takes the form of passionate and passible love in a kenotic vision of ultimate reality.

Luther's theology of the cross has become a key factor in revising the trinitarian paradigm. The triune God and the crucified Jesus belong together. The identification of God with the crucified Jesus requires that theology be serious about the trinitarian distinctions in God as Father, Son, and Holy Spirit. Then it no longer makes sense to speak of God in a simple untrinitarian way. It is the Son, Jesus of Nazareth, who suffers

and dies on the cross. But the Father suffers with him. Ancient patripas-
sionism was condemned because of its Sabellian unitarian presupposition. In a new trinitarian paradigm we may speak of the infinite grief of
the Father in the death of his Son, a real form of suffering as intense as
the suffering of dying.

   "God the Father" is a piece of language that derives its meaning
from its context and use. There is no sense denying that the symbol of
"Father" has a particular kind of meaning in the context of patriarchy,
wherein "Father" functions as a symbol of authority and domination all
up and down the scale of metaphysical, political, religious, and familial
relationships. But the symbol takes on another meaning in a covenant
context, wherein God becomes the Father of Israel by a historic act of
election, in contrast to the idea of generation in the pagan myths. "The
certainty that God is Father and Israel his son is grounded not in my-
thology but in a unique act of salvation by God, which Israel had experienced in history."[65] Jesus' use of "Father" language is intimately linked
to his preaching of the kingdom of God. A careful analysis of the biblical
context of meaning of "Father" will sound not only the note of patriarchy
but the notes of covenant and kingdom as well, which add up to a trans-
valuation of its meaning, as with the "basileia" symbol itself.

   A further step of language analysis discloses that, in the cultic context of primitive Christianity, the "Father" symbol loses its metaphorical
load of meaning associated with patriarchy and masculine characteristics
and begins to be used as proper name, together with Son and Holy
Spirit. The dictionary defines a proper name as "a name designating a
specific person." In his reflections on *la paternité*, Ricoeur suggests we
should give "zero content to the figure of father before daring to invoke
God as 'Father.' "[66] In Christian baptism, the name of God is invoked,
and that name (singular) is "Father, Son, and Holy Spirit." That is the
given Christian name of God, as JHWH is the proper name of God in the
Old Testament. The Hebrews believed that God revealed to them his
proper name by which to invoke him, and, since then, scholars have
been trying to decipher just what that name might mean. A person may
originally receive a proper name because of some meaningful association—clearly the case with many interesting American Indian names—
but once the proper name is given, the name no longer means anything.
It is a sheer appellation or name tag by which a person is known, called,
or spoken to in the framework of dialogue or personal exchange.

"Father-Son-Spirit" is something more than a metaphor or a symbol, although each of these terms is also a symbol with its own history of meaning. But, as applied to God, "Father-Son-Spirit" is a proper name in our Christian language system, used originally as such in the context of worship, for example, as invocation. It should be clear, even from these few words, that the name of God as "Father-Son-Spirit" enjoys a different linguistic status from the names of God classically debated since Dionysius the Areopagite in the speculative language of attribution. Fear of idolatry has caused the speculative mind to correct the seeming inadequacy of attributing particular attributes to God (that God is simple, perfect, good, infinite, omnipotent, etc.) by pushing the *via negationis* to the extreme. Whatever the validity of this method, some people have become confused by applying the same linguistic surgery to the name of God, ending up with an unnameable something-or-other, similar to Dionysius's superessential nothingness. The Christian naming of God as "Father, Son, Spirit" is not the idolizing of God but an event that arises in response to God's self-communication in Jesus Christ in the power of the Holy Spirit.

3   Franklin Sherman

RETICENCE AND EXUBERANCE IN SPEAKING OF GOD

*T*his essay will refer to two contrasting modalities of God-language, those suggested in my title by the terms "reticence" and "exuberance." The former I will present as more modest in its claims than some of our usual ways of speaking about God, and the latter as more expansive. From an Aristotelian standpoint, this looks like a typical case of two extremes (one of deficiency and one of excess), between which virtue is to be sought in the golden mean. What I wish to maintain, however, *contra* Aristotle, is that in this case there is more wisdom in the extremes than in the *via media*.

My polemic is directed against the notion that we have available to us any *literal* language about God; that is, the assumption that there can be a one-to-one correspondence between our assertions and God's reality. I say this even though I accept the classical Christian doctrines as true. The question is not *whether* they are true but *how* they are true (or, otherwise put, not *what* they mean but *how* they mean).

What we do have available in our religious and theological language, I suggest, is something less than a literal one-to-one referring, on the one hand, and yet something much more than this, on the other hand. Let us explore something of what this means.

At the root of religious and revelational experience, we know that we are dealing with matters that can be expressed only in what has been called "tensive" language, language that has been stretched to accommodate or point to truths that cannot be conveyed in flat, propositional statements. This is due to the simple fact that we are dealing with the

Transcendent (or that the Transcendent is dealing with us). In Scripture, such tensive language involves not only a myriad of symbols, in the narrower sense of the term, that is, of specific appellations drawn from the natural or human sphere and applied to the divine ("O Lord, my Rock and my Redeemer"). It involves also whole structures of discourse such as myth, saga, narrative, poetry, parables, prayers, aphorisms, blessings, ecstatic outcries, apocalyptic fantasies—none of which has anything remotely like a propositional form. Even in Paul, who no doubt comes closest, in Scripture, to being a systematic theologian, we have a deeply self-involving and tensional form of language ("Wretched man that I am! Who will deliver me from this body of death?").

Yet when we formulate our theological propositions, we conveniently forget the pluriform linguistic base on which they rest. Theological language, all agree, is second-order language compared to the directly religious utterances (whether experiential or revelational) that it conceptualizes. How could it be that such a second-order language, which by definition is one step removed from the realities with which it deals, would provide a closer and less equivocal grasp on those realities than the first-order language?

What we tend to forget is that in all of our Christian thinking as well as our believing, we are "swimming over 70,000 fathoms," in Kierkegaard's phrase. Every theological assertion is a leap of faith; in no case are we dealing with the self-evident or the irrefutably demonstrable. To be a Christian, as Paul Holmer likes to put it, is to have a certain way of construing the world. There are alternative construals.[1]

What this means is that all religious language must be *evocative* if it is to function as religious language at all. By "evocative," I mean such as to call forth a response from the hearer and, especially, to create a sense of awe, of reverence, of mystery, of noneverydayness—in short, of everything that Rudolf Otto meant by "the numinous." There definitely is and there must be an emotional component in religious language; the early linguistic positivists were right on this score but wrong in denying it truth value for this reason. God-language is a matter not only of our rational and ratiocinative side but of the whole brain and the whole self.

Paul Tillich, as is well known, maintained that all religious language is symbolic. This is because all religious language is about the Transcendent, or our relationships to the Transcendent, and yet the only language that we have is that which is formed by (or, in the subsequent terms of structuralism, gives form to) our empirical existence. That which we know is thrown against the screen of the unknown, and thereby sheds light upon the latter, and yet at the same time is transformed by it. All religious language therefore participates in the "is/is not" dialectic. "The Lord 'is/is not' my shepherd": "is not," in any literal sense (doesn't really bear a crook, doesn't have dirty feet, etc.); "is," in a metaphorical sense, that is, is *like* a shepherd in certain specified or tacitly understood ways ("makes me lie down in green pastures," "leads me beside still waters"—more metaphors!).

When pressed, Tillich acknowledged that there must be one non-symbolic assertion about God, of which all the others are modifiers, so to speak. For Tillich, this assertion was that God is Being-itself (in other formulations: the Ground of Being; the Power of Being; the Ground of Being and Meaning; the Ground and Abyss of Being and Meaning). We cannot go into the ramifications of this Tillichian concept here, but we do want to ask: What kind of assertion is this, or what kind of use of language does it involve?

In form, it seems to me that this is essentially a *definition*. Indeed, it is an "ostensive" definition, that is, one of the very simplest kind, that accomplishes its purposes by "pointing" rather than by analysis or synonymy. Tillich, from this perspective, is simply announcing what he intends to mean by "God"; or, otherwise put, how he proposes to use the word. (Cf. Ludwig Wittgenstein: "The meaning is the use.")

But although in form merely a definition, Tillich's assertion that "God is Being-itself," so far as its content is concerned, is in fact a mighty theological/philosophical/ontological assertion. It is one, moreover, that brings together in a synoptic view the two main sources of our culture, Athens and Jerusalem. For what Tillich is asserting in this formulation is what he stated in other terms on the concluding page of his book *Biblical Religion and the Search for Ultimate Reality,* when he wrote: *"Against* Pascal I say: The God of Abraham, Isaac, and Jacob and the God of the philosophers is the same God."[2]

Tillich was very aware of the contrasts involved in "Hebrew thought compared with Greek," and in fact gives an overview of them in that very book. Yet he is so convinced a monotheist (cf. H. Richard Niebuhr, *Radical Monotheism and Western Culture*) that he cannot but believe that the One whom the philosophers seek, and with them all those more common folk who also "hope that they might feel after him and find him,"[3] is the same as the Holy One of Israel.

Please note that what is in question here is not the success or failure of the quest, or even the adequacy of the questers' notions of what they are questing for, but rather the identification of the Object of the quest with the God whom we know, through Scripture, as the Self-revealing Subject. Truly an audacious step—yet one taken, apparently, long before Tillichian times, by the author of that Luke/Acts passage: "What therefore you worship as unknown, this I proclaim to you." Furthermore, it is a step possibly taken by Paul himself, if we can take his words in Romans 1 at anything like face value (which admittedly is difficult to do in this post-Barthian age): "For what can be known about God is plain to them, because God has shown it to them."[4]

Again, the point is not how great or little, how clear or cloudy is this knowledge or even whether it leaves the knower in a worse or better state (according to Paul, it serves only to confirm the knowers' guilt). Rather, what is of interest is the remarkable linguistic fact that Paul can use the same term, *theos,* to refer both to this God-in-general of the Gentiles and to the very specific God of the gospel that he proclaims.

Much depends upon whether we follow Tillich in making this linkage, thus being clear about the identity of the God we worship as not a tribal deity but truly the *Deus pater omipotens, creator coeli et terrae.* (More on the *pater* later.) A phrase like "Ground of Being," as applied to God, has often been taken to be reductive, probably because of its seeming impersonality. But God, for Tillich, and of course for the whole tradition of the *Deus omnipotens, Pantokrator,* is the Ground both of personal and of nonpersonal being, and hence deeply personal—but not merely "a" person. Properly understood, Tillich's formulation is a way of protecting the divinity of the divine.

If such is our God and Israel's God—a God "high and lifted up"— can such a God, we must now ask, really have a proper name? Or is it not the case that such a God must either have no name at all, or else a thousand names?[5]

On the face of it , this would seem to be not only a bold assertion but also a manifestly foolish and unscriptural one, for is it not the case that Exodus 3 tells us clearly that God revealed his name to Moses? But consider further the import of that narrative. It is Moses, not God, who initiates the dialogue: "If I come to the people . . . and they ask me, 'What is his name?' what shall I say to them?" God (Elohim) replies: I AM WHO I AM. Or, I AM WHAT I AM. Or, I WILL BE WHAT I WILL BE. Whichever rendering is adopted, surely what this amounts to, on the face of it, is a refusal to answer the question! "You ask my name, and thereby you wish to learn the secret of my identity, and perhaps even to gain power over me. But I will not make it that easy for you. All that I will tell you is that I am who I am; and furthermore, I will be what I will be. For further information, keep tuned, and listen for specific words of admonition, instruction, and grace; and above all, judge me by my deeds." Thus God too (or the ancient tradition that underlies this text) is concerned to protect the divinity of the divine.

Suppose, however, we were to take this as a name (a nameless name, so to speak)—what is its content? It is truly striking that it is, as I believe the majority of scholars posit, a variant on the verb "to be." It does not refer to any specific attribute of God; it does not present God as the God of power, or of love, or of fertility, or of this or that mountain, this or that tribe. All those specifications may be affirmed or denied in their proper place, and in an adjectival manner. Some of them, indeed, are set forth in this very context. But as to God's own most basic reality, that is, the *Fundament* of which much may subsequently be predicated, it is presented here (again, quite a few years prior to Tillich), precisely in terms of *be-ing*. The Septuagint translation is revealing: "And God *(ho theos)* said to Moses, EGO EIMI HO ON."

If this produces an aura of mystery, if it seems to raise more questions than it answers, then I say: good. Then we are perhaps on our way to speaking of a God who is truly God. A proper name does not do this. The ancient and modern (Orthodox) Jewish unwillingness to speak this name which extends even, with some, to an unwillingness to write the English word "God" (they spell it "G-d") is not, at its root, I suggest, a matter of fear of the name's magical effects (to cite a common interpretation). Rather, it is a way of signaling the divine transcendence, of avoiding even a suggestion that we can contain or manipulate the Deity.

There is a striking passage in Dietrich Bonhoeffer that refers to a similar reluctance to speak the name of God, though in a special context:

> I often ask myself [he writes to Eberhard Bethge in his letter of April 30, 1944] why a "Christian instinct" often draws me more to the religionless people than to the religious, by which I do not mean with an evangelizing intention, but, I might almost say, "in brotherhood" [we today might say: "in solidarity"]. While I am often reluctant to mention God by name to religious people—because that name somehow seems to me here not to ring true, and I feel myself to be slightly dishonest (it is particularly bad when others start to talk in religious terms;

I then dry up almost completely and feel awkward and uncomfortable)—to people with no religion I can on occasion mention him by name quite calmly and as a matter of fact.[6]

In terms of the alternatives that I set forth at the outset, to attempt to speak of God too directly, as if we could make literal statements about God just as we can about any existent object, is not to speak of God at all. God, as I have sometimes said in teaching introductory theology, is a *dimensional* reality. Therefore the dimension of the divine (or, the depth dimension; or, a sense of the numinous) must be evoked before the speaker can be in a position really to refer to God, or the hearer to receive the utterance as such. Thus, "No denotation without evocation."

My assumption, regarding Bonhoeffer, is that in a secular context he felt that the mere mention of God was so startling that in itself it evoked this sense of wonder (perhaps in the guise of incredulity), whereas among pious folk the religious coinage had been worn so smooth that it had lost all evoking *or* referring value.

With this I would connect up Kierkegaard's idea of "indirect communication," that is, that there are some things that by their very nature—having to do with the mystery of the Transcendent—are better hinted at than stated directly. To think that we possess these things too certainly is perhaps not to possess them at all. At one point Kierkegaard writes, in a vein not unlike that of Bonhoeffer in the passage just cited:

> Because everyone knows it, the Christian truth has gradually become a triviality, of which it is difficult to secure a primitive impression. This being the case, the art of communication at last becomes the art of *taking away,* of luring something away from someone. . . . When a man has his mouth so full of food that he is prevented from eating, and is likely to starve in consequence, does giving him food consist in stuffing still more in his mouth, or does it consist in taking some of it away, so that he can begin to eat?[7]

The example is a crude one, but I must say that I resonate to these words, especially in terms of what I feel is a malady that is afflicting us today, particularly the realm of worship. This is what I call "symbolic overload": the piling on of hymns, chants, lessons, litanies, anthems, prayers, confessions, creeds, and recitations of the history of salvation—any one of which would be immensely edifying if taken by itself and truly meditated upon, but when taken all together, create a severe case of symbolic indigestion. In my opinion, we are simply heaping the plate too full.

From this standpoint, one of the most welcome developments in recent years has been the introduction of periods of silence into the liturgy.[8]

So, in this sense I am calling for reticence in the use of symbols (cf. Mies van der Rohe: "less is more"). But at the same time, and I trust without inner contradiction, if anyone insists on certain symbols for God and those symbols only, then I become a champion of exuberance, lest the assumption of a one-to-one relation between word and reality reduce us, again, to the level of literalism. The principle still holds good: No denotation without evocation.

It is considerations such as these, as well as an ongoing concern to be as fair and accurate as possible in any comparisons we make between Christianity and Judaism, that determine my attitude toward the question of father-language as applied to God. Let me set this forth in terms of a number of propositions:

1. The term "Father" is so deeply rooted in the usage of Jesus, as well as of the New Testament as a whole, that we cannot but give it the greatest possible deference. Such deference can only be qualified, and not negated, by our contemporary sensibilities.

2. Historical texts cannot be changed. We cannot make the Lord's Prayer read: "Our Father and Mother . . . " any more than we can make Lincoln's Gettysburg Address begin: "Eighty-seven years ago . . . ." Such texts must either be used as they stand or else not at all.

3. The extent of Jesus' use of father-language may not be as great as it seems, however, if we study the Gospels one by one and consider the probable influence of the writers or redactors. It is noteworthy that by far the greatest number of such usages appear in the Fourth Gospel, with its deliberately constructed christological monologues and dialogues, which, though they undoubtedly reflect a genuine strain of early Christian piety, can certainly not be taken as *ipsissima verba*.[9]

4. The use of the term "Father" for the Deity was not unknown in the Judaism of Jesus' day; quite the contrary. As Robert Hamerton-Kelly points out in his valuable study *God the Father*,[10] Rabbi Johanan ben Zakkai, who is revered as one of the chief founders of rabbinic Judaism, favored the appellations "our heavenly Father" and "Israel's heavenly Father." It was very likely due to his influence that the term "Father" entered so deeply into the prayer and worship life of subsequent Judaism.[11]

5. Therefore "Father" cannot be, so to speak, the copyrighted Christian name for God; it cannot be that which uniquely distinguishes our conception of God, at least not over against Judaism.

6. In any case, "Father" is not merely a name but an appellation (as I have been calling it); or even more precisely, in grammarians' terminology, an *appellative*.[12] A proper name in the strict sense does not convey any information about the one named; it is merely a "pointer" to the one about whom then some assertion may be made. To call God "Father," however, conveys a great deal and is meant to do so.

7. Thus to address God as Father or to refer to God as such is to make a compressed confession, just as we do every time we use the phrase "Jesus Christ." "Our Father . . . " as an address to God in prayer means: "O God, whom we make bold, following Jesus' precept and example, to address as Father . . ." just as to use the phrase "Jesus Christ" means to declare that it is he whom we confess to be the Christ.

8. For all these reasons, if one is forced to choose between whether "Father" as applied to God is to be regarded as a symbol or a name, from my standpoint it must be regarded as a symbol. However, my use of the term "appellation" or "appellative" is intended to provide a middle category which indicates that it is frequently *a symbol functioning as a name*. As such, it must be honored; but its use is not indispensable in all circumstances, and it can be complemented by a variety of other symbol names.

9. The church's usage has not, in fact, canonized "Father" as the exclusive name for God, but on the contrary has followed a pluralistic mode. This is evident if we consider, for example, the collects for the Sundays in Lent; note the varied forms of address:

— "O Lord God"
— "Lord God, our strength"
— "Heavenly Father"
— "Eternal Lord"
— "God of all mercy"
— "Almighty God"

10. If it be claimed that it is the doctrine of the Trinity that has specially sanctified the Father-language, again, we can acknowledge the historical weight of this fact and the consequent deference that we must give to it. But Father-Son language is *not* the only way of speaking of the tripersonal God. Compare the usage enshrined in Luther's catechism: God as Creator, Redeemer, and Sanctifier. Or the riot of trinitarian images provided by early Christian writers: for example, God as the Root, the Shoot, and the Fruit (Tertullian); God as the Maker, the Mediator, and the Matter of Christians' graces (Origen).

11.   If, for reasons of contemporary sensibility (which I affirm), we want, not to *avoid* the use of "Father," but perhaps to reduce the incidence of its usage and, surely, to complement it with other images, it is important to find functional equivalents (to use the language of translation theory) for what the image of Father has conveyed. What I have in mind here are such meanings as:

— the One from whom we take our origin
— the Nurturing One
— the Protector
— the Disciplinarian
— the Refuge and Comforter

In contemporary society, the image of Mother may well convey much of this very range of meanings, and there is no a priori reason to shun its usage, as long as it is clearly understood as a symbol.[13]

12.   Therefore, with regard to this matter we should apply our twin criteria of reticence and exuberance. However meaningful a term may be to oneself or to the traditions that we cherish, it may be better not to use it, or to restrict its usage, if it causes one of the sisters or brothers to stumble. (Cf. Paul's self-denying ordinance in 1 Cor. 8:13, which he imposed on himself despite the fact that he was perfectly convinced that the objectors to meat-eating were mistaken.) Better, however, to take a positive tack—my "exuberance" strategy—and surround it with a plenitude of other terms and symbols that will complement it and at the same time allow its distinctive contribution to be clear.

Karen Bloomquist

"LET GOD BE GOD": THE THEOLOGICAL NECESSITY OF DEPATRIARCHALIZING GOD

*F*rom a feminist theological perspective, the question of God and God-language is not an abstract philosophical issue to be debated from a position of disinterested neutrality. It is first and foremost a moral issue, deeply entwined in our relationships with ourselves, others, and the world in which we find ourselves. Because human persons are essentially social, in a way that patriarchal consciousness has often overlooked, we cannot talk about the relationship between God and human persons apart from our relationships with one another, including the social constructs and ideologies by which those relationships are structured.

The past and continuing litany of women who have been silenced, rendered invisible, demeaned, raped, and dismembered provokes what for many feminists is the central God-question: Who is the God in whom we can believe? This theological quest arises out of moral outrage at what has been done to women throughout history in the name of "God," including in our own day. The director of a shelter for battered women told some of our students that in that community the chief instrument used to batter women is the Bible. It is used to justify any means to subordinate women to men. The "God" who has been used to justify or overlook such brutality will simply not suffice. To insist that God is not like that, while "he" continues to be referred to in ways that reinforce the power relations of patriarchy, is contradictory. That there *is* a God who has upheld, redeemed, and sustained women through their pain and struggle is for most women a given. Although some feminists may give attention to atheism as the problem, the God-question for most women is more similar to Luther's well-known quest for a God who is gracious, for a God who is liberative rather than oppressive.

Who is the God in whom women can believe? That is the question. Re-imaging and reworking understandings of God from such a persective have the potential to become another major "reformation," as threatening to the ecclesial-theological establishment as was the previous one, and themed with the same cry, "Let God be God." That is the real issue at stake.

The failure to recognize what really is at stake in the feminist challenge is revealed in a typical response of many men. They agree (grudgingly perhaps) to "clean up their language" so as not to "offend the women." If the women in "my" congregation or in "my" family" are not offended by "my" language, then it is assumed there is no onus to change. The very way in which the issue is set up belies the patriarchal assumptions that are operating. The men are in the positions of authority to be the final arbiters. It is "their" language and "their" women who are at stake, with the ownership assumption only thinly veiled. Attempts are made to "please" and not "offend" the women, that is, basic rules of etiquette must be observed so as to keep the underlying power relations of patriarchy in place.

Furthermore, what this position overlooks is that many women have been as blinded and silenced by the assumptions of a patriarchal system as have men. The complacency of many women with the way the social structure and God-language within it operate, rather than dismissing the need for fundamental change, points instead to the deep and urgent need for such change. Changing the language not only is necessary in those settings where feminists consciously pressure for such but it is especially urgent where there is no such outcry, that is, where patriarchal assumptions continue to silence, mystify, and victimize ordinary women.

What is involved is more than excavating the biblical-theological understandings of God that would counter such misuses. Although necessary, this is not sufficient because of how texts, images, and God-language come to function in the subsequent life of a community. Symbols develop a life or history of their own, which must be dealt with as well as the original meaning. The original meaning can help to challenge our contemporary understandings, but the "normative" meaning of a biblical position will result from a dialectic of the original and the present "meaning horizons".[1]

For our purposes here, pervasive in that meaning horizon is the reality of patriarchy. In addition to its narrow definition in terms of the specific *pater familias* structure, patriarchy can more generally be defined as a male-dominant power structure in a society in which all relationships are understood in terms of superiority or inferiority, and social cohesion is assured by the exercise of dominative power.[2] Within patriarchy, males and females are politically differentiated, not as individuals but as members of a social class. Sexual difference becomes the excuse for gender inequality. Females are subjected to the male construct of "femininity," implying females' relinquishment of power or the indirect or manipulative exercise of power.[3] Patriarchy is essentially dualistic and hierarchical. The power and the authority exercised over subordinates are believed to derive from God's will and are exercised in the name of "God." The subordination is difficult to protest without appearing to challenge God "himself." Patriarchy is the basic principle underlying sexism, racism, classism, colonialism, and other institutionalized patterns of inequality. Inequality of power becomes embedded in how we view reality and in how we do theology.

The social structures and ideologies of patriarchy permeate a society's language. Language is not merely an external feature of reality, but as the major traditions of social theory have asserted in recent decades, language is the main bearer and transmitter of the social structure. It encodes our sense of how we are related to others, with patterns of domination and subordination implicit in it. The language itself is revelatory of unjust relations.

God-language bespeaks a whole social structure. In a patriarchal society, the pyramidal structure typically has God on top, then, in hierarchical order, men, women, children, and nature. As a theologian I would insist that God-language does more than legitimize a given social order, but I cannot discount those conscious and unconscious ways in which it does precisely that. Insofar as the social structure has valued males more than females, from a feminist moral perspective it must be challenged. Challenging the God-language operative within that structure is at the core of this moral struggle. As Elisabeth Moltmann-Wendel states:

> The image of God as Father had been useful for forming personality in a patriarchal society. In a hierarchy it offered protection and privacy,

trust and security. For a changing society which is apparently fatherless and has undergone a process of internalizing patriarchal laws, images and ideas are needed to replace the restrictive patriarchal morality which puts women in their place.[4]

Tillich's familiar understanding of "symbol" is that it participates in the reality for which it stands and in the power to which it points.[5] The segment of finite reality, in this case male experience, which becomes a vehicle of concrete assertions about God, is affirmed and negated at the same time. Males are like God, but not like God. If God is symbolized as "Father," God is concretized in terms of the human relationship of father and child. *At the same time*, this human relationship is consecrated into a pattern of the divine-human relationship, thereby giving fatherhood theonomous, sacramental depth. If a segment of reality is used as a symbol for God, that realm is elevated into the realm of the holy.[6] Once it becomes "holy," it becomes untouchable, not to be tampered with or changed. In trying to communicate what God is *like*, we use symbols that then tend to be perceived as God-like. If we are to speak of the God revealed through the Bible, we cannot avoid using human vehicles, but a more balanced variety of symbols rather than nearly exclusively male ones can help circumvent the tendency to divinize the male at the expense of the female.

Retrieving, Rejecting, Reworking

There are three basic feminist approaches to our central inquiry: Who is the God in whom we can believe? One is primarily engaged in *retrieving* the nonpatriarchal aspects of our biblical-theological tradition that have been there all along, although often overlooked. Another has *rejected* the historic faith of Jewish and Christian communities, insisting that it is too pervasively and essentially patriarchal to be worth saving. Efforts are devoted instead to retrieving or creating religious traditions that are nonpatriarchal and empowering of women. A third accepts how pervasively patriarchal the tradition is, but insists that it is not essentially so and hence is engaged in the complicated project of *reworking* the symbols and understandings of the faith from out of a nonpatriarchal, that is, feminist, perspective.

Those identifying with the "retrieval" approach would insist that there is basically no incompatibility between women's quest for justice and wholeness and the biblical-theological tradition. The latter inspires and sustains the former. While they acknowledge that sexist biases have tainted many translations, interpretations, and practices, clearing up such biases so that the consistency between the biblical-theological tradition and women's contemporary quest for justice can shine through is seen as a relatively clear, straightforward task. Guiding motifs in this endeavor are the creation of male and female in God's image, the baptismal "new creation" in Jesus Christ, in whom there is neither male nor female,[7] and the recorded accounts of Jesus' amazingly egalitarian dealings with women, which establish for some contemporary interpreters that indeed "Jesus was a feminist."[8] Searching for the women who have been "lost" or overlooked in Bible and church history, and for the hidden feminine images and metaphors for God, is part of the retrieval project.

The basic position here is that there is no inherent problem in "adding women and stirring" because the tradition is at root nonsexist. Although often clouded by patriarchal trappings, these have not distorted the central theological understandings. Clearing up the past misunderstandings that have been perpetuated should be sufficient to enable the Bible's freeing message to transform women today. The God in whom feminists can believe is basically the God whom the church has proclaimed all along. It is mandatory that this God be proclaimed in such a way as to make it totally unambiguous that women are as fully included as are men in the divine intention. It would be helpful if language and imagery for God were more female-oriented, enabling women more readily to relate their experience to God. However, not all retrieval feminists would insist that this is *essential*, because of the central presumption that the God revealed through albeit patriarchal Judaic and Christian traditions has nevertheless, when rightly understood, communicated "good news" for women. Patriarchy, although pervasive, has not infected the basic substance of Christian thought.

This position was characteristic of the beginnings of feminist theology in the early 1970s among especially committed church women, and was the beginning of a contemporary challenging of the ways in which androcentric theological traditions have silenced and rendered women invisible. (The connection between religious thought and male/female power was earlier made by nineteeth-century feminists.) It was the experience of being excluded that provided the motivating impetus for this theological endeavor. The goal was that of clearing away the rubbish in order to uncover the ground on which self-respecting women could stand and be fully "included in" again. The problem was that those of us

who engaged in this endeavor in the early 1970s were not yet cognizant
of how pervasively the rubbish of patriarchy had penetrated and pol-
luted the ground on which *all* (not only women) depend for their suste-
nance, necessitating not just a cleanup operation but a major excavation
and landscaping project.

This far more radical challenge was set forth by those who now are
seen as "post-Christian or post-Jewish" feminist theologians, most notably Mary Daly:

> If God in "his" heaven is a father ruling "his" people, then it is in the
> "nature" of things and according to divine plan and the order of the
> universe that society be male-dominated.[9]

What Daly argues is that our entire system of theology and ethics, developed under conditions of male dominance, has been a product of patriarchy and has served sexist interests. The symbols and traditions of
Christianity are inherently and essentially sexist. In her later books, she
maintains that the tenets and symbols of patriarchal religion have been
consciously designed to justify male control and to foster hatred toward
women.

In response to those feminists who seek to demonstrate what a feminist Jesus was, Naomi Goldenberg replies, "So what?" The point is that
regardless of how liberating and egalitarian he was toward women, the
Christ symbol since then has become an oppressive symbol for women,
such that "he" cannot symbolize liberation for women. What the spokes-
persons for this "rejecting" approach propose is that women need to
make a clear break and enter a new space where harmonious noncon-
tradictory visions and traditions can be spun, whether that means going
back to retrieve the Goddess and other religious impulses that have been
declared heretical, or developing new myths, language, and traditions.

If we too quickly condemn or undercut these critiques and alternative proposals, we betray our own bondage to patriarchal ways of operating (i.e., by "shooting down the other"). We repeat the age-old way
that women have been dealt with, namely, by condemning as heretical
those strains which have broken out from under the usual patterns of
male dominance. In other words, we prove the point that these radical
feminists are trying to make and lend fuel to the argument that the symbols of Christianity are inherently sexist.

The third approach in feminist theology takes seriously the critique
that the "rejecting" approach makes of "the tradition." It acknowledges

how pervasively patriarchal the tradition is but insists that the tradition has done something else besides legitimating sexism. Those of us identifying with this position find that we have been grasped by a liberating dynamic within the tradition that has somehow broken through in spite of all the patriarchal constructs. There has been something besides patriarchy that has gotten through to women for all these years, convincing some of us that indeed there is Word of *God* and not merely words of *men* embedded in the biblical theological witness.

Therefore the task is that of "reworking" the symbols and understandings of the faith so that they no longer are captive to patriarchal interests. This involves challenging the patriarchal distortions from the inside by using key resources within that tradition itself and yet interpreting these resources so that the tradition begins saying things that haven't been heard before. There is an insistence that no social group can set itself up against others as image and agent of God or use God to justify social domination.[10] The patriarchy of certain metaphors is assumed because of the culture, but the message of the metaphors subverts patriarchy.[11]

This task is empowered by a fundamental faith in a divine power that cannot be confined to any social structure, specifically in a God (or Goddess) who "transcends" patriarchy. As Celie insists in *The Color Purple*, "You have to git man off your eyeball before you can see anything a'tall." Yet the Deity cannot be imaged or spoken of apart from some social assumptions. Ideology and faith are far more deeply intertwined than has usually been assumed. Form and meaning are difficult if not impossible to extricate from one another. But as we begin to interpret the faith through an ideological lens that is an alternative to patriarchy, in the clash between those two world views, what is essential can perhaps be glimpsed.

Reworking the Biblical-Theological Tradition

How have patriarchal assumptions been incorporated into our most basic ways of thinking and talking about God? Understanding the implications of recent feminist scholarship on the origin of patriarchy is important in helping us identify the dimensions of what needs to be addressed in this theological task. The common tenet of such scholarship is that patriarchy emerged in history; it is not an ontological given, despite its seeming universality. Male dominance as a historical phenomenon was based on certain biologically determined givens but became a culturally created and enforced structure over the time span of approximately twenty-five hundred years.[12] By the time men began symbolically to order the universe and the relation of human beings to God, the subordination of women had become "natural" to both men and women.[13]

There are differences in identifying how patriarchy began or what kind of social order it succeeded. A few scholars have posited a prehistorical matriarchy, but many dispute this, suggesting instead a more ambiguous prehistory with no real ascendancy of one gender over the other. The presence of mother-goddess figures in a number of early societies, although suggesting the positive valuation of female power, does not by itself presume a matriarchal social structure.

As to why patriarchy arose, an emerging consensus among a variety of feminist scholars in anthropology, history, and philosophy, as well as theology, is that it arose as a compensation for men's physiological inability to give birth. In early societies, giving birth connoted a divine power, especially when the male role in procreation was not yet known. Females, in being able to reproduce themselves, exhibited greater permanence and were experienced as having the key to immortality in a way that males did not. Thus, males experienced females as a substantial ego threat. Azizah al-Hibri, a feminist philosopher, theorizes that males' desire and struggle for the "immortality" that women seemed to have is why males developed ways of appropriating women and their "sacred" life-giving power.[14] He appropriates her, that is, her sexuality and reproduction, such that she becomes commodified, that is, his private property. Maleness came to connote power, strength, and positive agency, so that the male could ensure "his" women and progeny as his own.

In this process, males also acquired hegemony over the symbol system and transformed the major symbols of female power into symbols of male procreativity. For example, the focus shifts to the male's "seed," assumed to be complete in itself, needing the female only for incubation. (This continues to be the unexamined premise in some antiabortion positions today.) Although Hebrew religion is often viewed as a move away from the fertility religions of the Canaanites, the suggestion has been set forth that the fertility emphasis still remained, only transformed into male terms, specifically through circumcision as the sign of dedication to the one God and "his" blessing of male procreativity.[15]

The genesis of the Western patriarchal, masculine God occurred alongside the subjugation of women, who, in this new paradigm, were seen as tempting men away from righteousness and the immortality for which women had previously been the agents. Cross-cultural anthropological studies indicate that it is the combination of masculine religious symbols in a society and a climate of social stress and competition that endorses male dominance.[16] Control and dominance are seen as necessary in the face of fear, conflict, and strife. If a people's identity is forged in less adverse circumstances, and hence less dependent on aggressive acts of men, the gender power relations are likely to be different.[17] Gender power relations change when the situation is such that without change things would come apart, which in our day may suggest a move away from the qualities associated with male dominance.

Perspectives such as these on the origin of gender inequality and of the symbol systems related to such provoke uncomfortable questions of suspicion, especially regarding the structure of theological thought and thus of God-language.

The emergence of Hebrew monotheism, and hence the exclusion of goddess figures, has been linked with the emergence of dualistic understandings of sexuality.[18] The independent image of women is taken over, even demonized. Male control over women becomes the analogy for divine control over human beings. There is one in charge, and "he" is male. If "he" is the creator of life by himself, within this monotheistic patriarchal framework, creation can only be *ex nihilo*. The point is not that these were conscious, deliberate moves to link the roots of our faith to patriarchal frameworks, nor is it to overlook that some matriarchal qualities did carry over, but it is to suggest that whatever the theological intentions, reinforcing the dynamics of patriarchy was one of the key social functions of the dualistic, hierarchical theological thought and imagery that began to emerge.

Four interrelated aspects of how God is conceptualized are, from a feminist perspective, particularly suspect because they are ways of thinking and talking about God that are essentially patriarchal:

1. In Western theological thought, God is often conceived of *dualistically*. "He" and the world are dichotomized. The transcendent is dichotomized from the immanent, spirit from matter, the creator from creatures, and a masculine God from "feminized" believers. Gender becomes the underlying dualism on which these dichotomies are erected.

There are numerous examples in Scripture where such dichotomies are not seen as necessary in order to communicate who God is and what God is about. A major witness against such dualisms is the incarnation.

The uniting of the divine and the human is a radical scandal that the church has always had difficulty with. The "either/or" logic of patriarchal consciousness cannot conceive of a "both/and" option. As Patricia Wilson-Kastner proposes, all the dualisms that divide, separate, cause pain, and support oppression rather than community are gathered together at the cross. Those qualities most incompatible—most dualistic— are paradoxically united in the Crucified One. In redemption, dualisms are overcome.[19]

2. *Hierarchical* categories are often viewed as necessary in communicating that God is God, that is, in maintaining God's transcendence. The question is, Can God be God without the necessity of hierarchically ordered relationships? Hierarchy is often viewed as divinely instituted, but many feminists would challenge this. To make God dependent on hierarchical patterns is to limit God to what is humanly contrived. In this sense, insistence on the use of hierarchical patterns in doctrine and language regarding God is itself idolatrous:

> God the monarch, supremely free and sovereign over "his" created, is
> a conception of domination. Only God is free under this rubric, and
> the people are "his" property.[20]

The biblical notion of a God who is personally accessible and who enters into loving, steadfast relationships with people can best be communicated through more mutually relational categories. A hierarch tends to be distant, separate, ruling over "his" people in a way that deters the emergence of genuine relation. In contrast, Jesus' experience was of a God who is in intimate, immediate relation with him.

3. Those who would cling to hierarchy as a way of expressing God's transcendence also are challenged by feminist critiques of understandings of God's *power*. For many feminists, power is not a fixed quantity, such that one having more power means the other has less power. Power need not be viewed as "control over" but as that which enables and empowers others. The transcendent God is often imaged as a power of hierarchical relation, an almighty God, the essence of whose power is control. That, insists Carter Heyward, is a use of power that is neither creative nor redemptive. A deity who exercises power as control over those who have only to trust and obey blindly is a problematic understanding of transcendence. It results in a Christianity that reflects

an enormity of control in its preaching and practices—but a dearth of benevolence, justice, and mercy—whether on the mission fields or in the bedroom. . . . Faith in a divine master of domination and control . . . [serves] to safeguard our claims as those of an all-powerful "God" and our values as reflective of all that he values on earth.[21]

Furthermore, such a use of "transcendence" is contrary to what "transcend" literally means, namely, to cross over, to bridge, or to make connections. A truly transcendent God knows the bounds of no human life or location but is always too actively crossing over boundaries to become any group's source of special privilege. We have "stuck God" with a notion of transcendence that is a projection of those who are used to being in charge.

Consequently, by dichotomizing transcendence and immanence we overlook that transcendence is a relational power that moves to cross over from person to person, race to race, class to class, gender to gender, binding us into one body, breaking down all that would keep us apart. That power is transcendent precisely in its immanence among us.[22]

4. Finally, the net effect of the above three tendencies is to conceive of God in "his" *aloneness*, as if that is what makes God divine:

If "He" is set apart from human experience (physical, tangible, sensual, painful, humorous, delightful, terrible experience in the world) by the nature of "His" impassivity, then God is completely useless to us. Such a "God" is a destructive, controlling device, manufactured in the minds of men who have bent themselves low before ideals of changeless Truth, deathless Life, pure Spirit, perfect Reason, and other qualities often associated with the patriarchal "God."[23]

Aloneness, impassibility, and autonomy are often characterized as the male stereotype in our society. What have we done in so masculinizing God? What God is like becomes equated with what males are conditioned to be like, thereby deluding themselves and others that they are "god-like."

The church's central doctrinal understanding of God—namely, the Trinity—is a strong voice against so conceiving God. God as the hierarchical ruler supposedly was repudiated when the church established the doctrine of the coeternality and coequality of the three members of the Trinity. A primary motive in trinitarian formulae was to secure Jesus' divinity. Hence, as Susan Brooks Thistlethwaite analyzes the situation, Christology tended to overtake pneumatology, replacing the Spirit with an impersonal, controlling grace that leaves believers passive rather than empowering them. The church becomes a spiritual realm animated by a pacifying and harmonizing Spirit that has no independent identity. Such a spiritual realm becomes privatized and divorced from the messy world and the conflicts in it. Thus we are left with a feminized Spirit to tend to the "private" realm, while Father and Son remain the active agents in the "public" realm.

Let us look more closely at what this gender duality has done to God. The Spirit, subordinate to the Father and even to the Son (in the Western church), confined to maintaining personal relationships with no independent identity of its own, ends up sounding stereotypically feminine in the extreme. Society has tended to assign women the responsibility for maintaining relationships, allowing men to view themselves as self-seeking, competitive, aggressive, and sustained by nurturing women:

> It is then not, perhaps, so curious that theologians have done the same to the Godhead. One aspect of God, an aspect deemed subordinate and peripheral, the Spirit, has been chosen to be responsible for self-giving and for sustaining relationships. But God the "Father" has remained the "Almighty": impassive, remote and unknowable, dominating "his" creation.[24]

Reclaiming the coequality of God the Spirit with God the Creator and Redeemer is necessary if the Spirit is to be seen as free to act in history and to do so through our relationships. God is essentially a relational God—how else could we proclaim "God is love"? God gives and God receives. Such give-and-take relationship is a sign not of weakness but of strength. Because we are culturally so hooked on the myth of the self-contained, self-possessed, autonomous man, such an image has also been projected onto God. Bonding with others, which tends to be associated with women, is seen as a sign of dependence, need, and weakness. Feminists would insist that that "ain't necessarily so!"

Insofar as our culture has devalued what is associated with women, so too we have devalued such in God. It is as a relational God that God's presence becomes most powerful in our lives and history, not as one who controls us but as one who empowers us. We become empowered to seek and live out just relationships that are mutually enriching and fulfilling, not ones that build up one party and the expense of the other.

Glimpses of this kind of relationality seem to be present in the Gospels' portrayal of Jesus. We cannot deny that he was male. He had status and privileges that he would not have had as a female in that society. But at crucial points he is depicted as going against the societal expectations, whether consciously or not. He refused to lord himself over others, particularly over women. The unquestioned connotations of gender, that is, the power of men over women, were challenged through the ways he related to women. He broke taboos prohibiting men from conversing with women to whom they were not related (the woman at the well). He refused to have any woman, including his own mother, identified primarily in terms of her childbearing function.[25] His relationships with women were not limited by women's prescribed role or status in society. His actions suggest a challenging of what is the most universal relationship of domination and submission—that between males and females. It was transformative relationships, not biological or social givens, which were primary in his life and hence in the meaning of who the Christ is for us today. Biology is not destiny. If the seemingly most absolute status began to be transformed through Jesus' historical activity, that breaks open new transformative possibilities for us—for men as well as for women.

In the Synoptics we find a Jesus who did not proclaim himself as king but who proclaimed the reign of God. In that promise he focused on the "little ones" whom especially the religious leaders of that day had excluded or trivialized. He called people not to subject themselves to the existing social order of bondage, but pointed instead to a new sense of God's saving activity revealed in their present while pointing to the future. We find a Jesus who willed the wholeness and humanity of everyone and who had a following—a Jesus movement—that was a discipleship of equals. Those who once had no hope now had hope.

Unfortunately these images of Jesus are a far cry from the Christ whom much of the church has proclaimed since then. As the early Christian movement grew and became more established, Christ tended to become a timeless revelation of divine perfection rather than an iconoclastic, prophetic figure to empower people in their present. In the fourth century, as the Constantinian era began, Christianity became installed with political power over the world. It became an imperial religion, providing a "sacred canopy" over the existing social order. Understandings of who Christ is became increasingly hierarchical and otherworldly. No longer was Christ viewed as one who frees from oppression. Christ was no longer encountered through slaves and women, but instead his maleness was accentuated in importance, to the point that only males could represent him, as continues to be the case to this day in Roman Catholicism. As Rosemary Radford Ruether contends, Christology became the apex of a system of control over all who are "other" and inferior in some way, particularly women. Christ was increasingly seen as the founder and cosmic governor of existing social hierarchies.

Certainly much of this carried over and continued to influence the Lutheran tradition. But there also is within this tradition a distinctive emphasis with the potential to challenge these tendencies. I refer to the "theology of the cross" emphasis. Luther insisted that God is not known through the visible or analogical means but through invisible and seemingly contradictory means. In what we regard as contrary to the divine—through such experiences as trouble, misery, and weakness—God becomes visible, and not through what human beings have created or assumed to be "of God" (which today would need to include such "isms" as racism and sexism and imperialism). Therefore:

1. The true God is not the omnipotent monarch but the one who divests "himself" of power, who hides under the opposite of what the world recognizes as omnipotence, who is the "crucified God." God is none other than the One manifest on the cross, revolutionizing our idea of God and of power.

2. The good news is not of deliverance *from* the experience of pain and struggle (removing us from it) but of permission to enter it with expectancy, and therefore with freedom. This is not masochism but an insistence that authentic liberation is found as we confront and enter into the negations and contradictions of our lives.

3. A theology of the cross proclaims a God whose will is to *be with us*, radically to identify with us in our concrete, everyday experience—in our suffering, in our femaleness, in our maleness, in the givenness of our particular situation.

4. Consequently, God is not preeminently revealed through the male-ensconced values of our society—especially those of mastery or power over others. The male-centered, patriarchal qualities attached to God are overturned. No more need there be an idolatrous projection upon God of the characteristics of the ruling sexual group. God's "otherness" is in terms of that which the predominant society has devalued.

Jesus is not a model for women to imitate, in some kind of scapegoat, self-sacrificing role. To identify with him in that sense would only increase our victimization and mutilation. We are not to give ourselves up to be crucified for anyone's sake but are "to struggle together against the injustice of all human sacrifice, including our own.[26]

The cross reveals to us intimations of the God who identifies with us in the cruciform sufferings that are already a part of our lives as women and thus encourages us to struggle against them. The cross challenges any triumphalistic link between God and the kind of exclusive "power over others" that controls, limits, and destroys women and others. That kind of power which has given divine sanction to racism, capitalism, imperialism, and sexism is challenged by the cross. Such "power over" has been central to the social understanding of what it means to be male in this society. To the extent that God through the cross is freed up from an identification with such dominating power, God is also freed up from the social criterion of maleness.

The christological symbol of receptivity to God's will and to self-sacrifice, if it had been historically embodied in a woman, would have only reinforced a not too helpful stereotype—that of the self-sacrificing female. If he had been a woman, he would have gotten even less of a hearing in his day than he did! Instead, Jesus, a male, through his interactions with others, helped to break the stereotype of who males are. He challenged the social definitions of power and hence of the power relationship between men and women. Mutual relationships rather than hierarchical relationships are what he lived out and to what he calls us today.

There is a richness in the self-revelation of God in Christ that discloses more inclusiveness than Christianity has dared to preach. An exclusive god created by men and encapsulated in male imagery of power and privilege must be challenged so that the true God can live. God encourages us to resist patriarchy's deathblows, to stand on our feet, empowered by the one we know as Christ who identifies fully with us. One of our students describes in powerfully moving terms her experience of being raped, and as she lay there on the ground fearing that she would be killed, what flashed before her was a vision of Christ—of Christ as a woman—"because only a woman would understand."

God is immanently with us, revealed through our pain and struggle, but "she" is more than immanent, more than female. God is always "other," moving us beyond simple identification with what is, thus endlessly challenging all of our human attempts to nail down God. God is the continually transforming horizon of human existence, calling us to break with patterns of oppression. God is always with us and always other. Salvation in Christ occurs through what happened on the cross, but the new creation that is set loose through the resurrection—the iconoclastic, transforming power of God—creates a new partnership, a new "us," a new church.

HOW ISRAEL
CONCEIVED OF AND
ADDRESSED GOD

*H*ow Israel conceived of and addressed God, and how God was conceived of and addressed in the Old Testament, are two quite distinct questions, and yet they obviously overlap and intersect, affecting each other in Old Testament times just as they do in our own thinking. That is to say, the faith embodied in the Old Testament texts is different from the "other" faith, the faith found among historical Israelites which peeks through the texts. Both kinds of faith reflect historical process and development, but the "faith of the Old Testament texts" may be described as the one that predominated, finally, and carried the traditions forward in canonical form. This present study can only dare to offer an impression, a mere profile of the information from the Old Testament on each question.

For Ibn Ezra (d. 1167 C.E.), the great rabbinic commentator, the commandment not to "take the name of Yahweh thy God in vain" was more important than all those that followed, because murder, adultery, and theft are all shaped by opportunity and fear, "but misuse of God's name, once it becomes a habit, will proliferate 'and in the end one's every assertion will be preceded by using the Name.' The result is a devaluation of awe and respect, and in time the holiness of God has no further meaning."[1] Although the dominant concern here seems to have been the too frequent use of the name, meaninglessly and pointlessly, beneath that concern lies a more profound issue: the relationship of the name(s) for God to our understanding of God and finally of everything else that we know.

Names for God, and How They Were Blended Together

In the Old Testament, and for Israel after centuries of history, the premier name for God was Yahweh. This name, in the beginning one of several by which the Deity was known, by some time at least as early as the early monarchy became preeminent and special among the other names, and finally late in the postexilic period it became so identified with God's being that it was not even used popularly. Already in Deuteronomistic circles (seventh century B.C.E.) the very word "name" (*šem*) connoted God's very presence—and of course "name" never meant anything except "Yahweh." In those theological circles Zion was the place where Yahweh had caused his name to dwell, and that raised it qualitatively above every other place; the theology of the "name," its power and its place, had become a primary issue for D. It is in the work of Isaiah of the exile, in Ezek. 36–43, in a large number of passages in Jeremiah that may have originated somewhat later than the prophet, and in Deuteronomy and the Deuteronomistic work that the specification of God's name Yahweh as Israel's theological hallmark became historically centered. This era, from shortly before until soon after the exile (i.e., the sixth century B.C.E.), must be regarded as a focal point both for the Old Testament and for Israel's history of God-language.

The traditions of the patriarchs bear a far different message from that of the sixth-century theologians, and the traditions transmitters freely carried that message down through history. In those traditions God had appeared and was known through many persons and places and by many variants of name. The Priestly tradition even bears its own explanation for a scheme of revelation of divine names. In Exod 6:2ff. we are told: "Then Elohim spoke to Moses, and he said to him, 'I am Yahweh'; and I appeared to Abraham, to Isaac, and to Jacob as El Shaddai, but by my name Yahweh I did not become known to them." In carrying out this story of revelation, the Priestly writers used the names Elohim and Yahweh throughout their work in the patriarchs but also introduced El Shaddai often enough (Gen. 17:1; 28:3, 35:11; 48:3)[2] to remind their readers of the governing pattern.

What *El Shaddai* might have meant is debated still today, after years of attention. *Shaddai* has been attributed to such diverse derivations as mountain, field, and devastation.[3] Jerome saw *omnipotens* (almighty) behind the term, and this of course underlies the common translation

"God Almighty"; the Septuagint translators were clearly confused by it in Genesis, but the translation of Job sometimes rendered *Shaddai* as Pantocrator (Almighty). El Shaddai occurs about thirty times in Job (out of fifty in the whole Old Testament), and Norman Habel suggests that for Job the etymology of the name was probably irrelevant anyway, because the poet of the book simply chose old titles.[4] Klaus Koch understands Shaddai in Job as "divine neighbor";[5] Bernhard Lang, citing others in support, regards it as expressing a personal guardian angel theology.[6] Amid this bewildering variety of suggestions, one thing that can probably be claimed is that El Shaddai is a term differing qualitatively from the "god of the fathers" language of the patriarchal period. El Shaddai seems to have had no connection with any special individual or any special place.[7]

In the earliest days of Israel's history a prominent feature in speaking of God seems to have been the association of the God with a person to whom the God had been revealed and who served the God. "The God of Abraham," "the Kinsman of Isaac," and "the Mighty One of Jacob" were terms with greater importance than their frequency of occurrence would suggest. Although these terms are found only very seldom in Genesis, they lie at the heart of the consciousness that a revelation had occurred to the ancestors and that a knowledge of God had been experienced. "God of the fathers" and its variants occur many times and in critical passages; it was Israel's way historically to relate the faith of later times to the ancestors of long ago and to the ancestral promises. Exodus 3:13-15 is an excellent example of how the traditions and names were linked together and blended:

> Then Moses said to the Elohim, "Behold, I'll be going to the children of Israel, and I shall say to them, 'The Elohim of your fathers [the word could be translated "parents" if there were no context to account for] has sent me to you,' and they will say to me, 'What is his name?' What will I say to them?" Then Elohim said to Moses, " '*ehyeh asher 'ehyeh*." And he said, "Thus shall you say to the children of Israel, '*ehyeh* sent me to you.' " And Elohim said furthermore to Moses, "Thus shall you say to the children of Israel, 'Yahweh, the Elohim of your fathers, the Elohim of Abraham, the Elohim of Isaac, and the Elohim of Jacob sent me to you. . . . Go, and gather the elders of Israel, and say to them, 'Yahweh, the Elohim of your fathers appeared to me, the Elohim of Abraham, Isaac and Jacob.' "

Examples like this (the very next one is in Exod. 4:5) are too numerous to mention. They serve to remind us that this tradition of naming

God stressed the relationship between God and individual persons and families, and linked the Yahweh tradition to beginnings that could be maintained in bold historical tension. Theologically we may say with Albrecht Alt that "the 'Gods of the fathers' were the *paidagōgoi* [guides, guardians] to the Great God who later on completely filled their place."[8]

There is question as to whether *Elohim* might ever have had a specific meaning. If anything, it may have been a generic term and served Hebrew theology well in that capacity. It permitted speaking of God in a general way, without necessarily rehearsing old themes or pointing out any particular identification or association. The so-called E material in Genesis (e.g., chaps. 20; 21; 22) preferred to call God Elohim. The Elohistic section of the Psalter (Pss. 42–83), and the portions of Chronicles that changed the text to Elohim in copying material from the Deuteronomistic historian of Samuel (who had used *Yahweh*), deliberately chose to alter the name for God, using Elohim when the antecedent material was obviously extant to demonstrate the older, alternate reading. They are evidence that some person(s) felt compelled, or free, to alter a text and tradition and preferred the generic *Elohim* to *Yahweh*.[9]

When Israel used El as a name for God, however—and it often occurred in passages that reflect the early period before the monarchy—a distinct set of associations came into play; for El was the father god and creator figure of the Canaanites.[10] El also could be used as a general name for god, one supposes, and is at least the root parallel to related forms found in a variety of Semitic languages. The forms combining El with some other element (El-Elyon, El-Olam, El-Roi, El-Bethel, and El-Berith, along with El-Shaddai) very probably conveyed associations with the old Canaanite figure, and surely this was the case in the El-Elyon passage in Genesis 14. It has been commonly observed that El seems not to have been regarded as a competitive figure against Yahweh, and the absorption of its qualities into the figure of Yahweh appears to have occurred rather effortlessly in Israel.[11] Evidently the Yahwists were not threatened by Canaanite ideas about El which did not constitute a negating of or deny vital claims about Yahweh. Perhaps an easy blending or joining of ideas about creation facilitated the process.[12] In any case, there seems to have been no fundamental barrier in Israel to calling Yahweh El and to inviting into the Yahweh figure some qualities and associations attached to El.

This early relating—one might almost say collapse—of divine names into one figure and common terminology was not the experience between Yahweh and Baal in the faith of the Old Testament traditions; but in the Israelites' experience this surely must have been the case. In popular understanding, much activity of Yahweh was difficult to distinguish from that of Baal. The figure of Baal in Canaanite religion—the god of fertility and war, rains and procreation, as well as the victor over death's forces in the struggle within nature, and therefore on all counts in vital touch with life and its maintenance—would have been highly competitive with Yahweh. Children were named Bealiah ("Yahweh is Baal," 1 Chron. 12:5) and Beeliada ("Baal knows," a name of David's son, 1 Chron. 14:7). When this first became an obvious problem cannot be ascertained. It surely was a threat for Hosea, however, and when he had a dream for Israel's future well-being it was, "And in that day, utterance of Yahweh, you will call me 'My husband (*'iš*).' and you will not call me any longer 'my Baal' " (Hos. 2:16). The contest between Elijah and the prophets of Baal on Mt. Carmel a century before Hosea marks the early highwater mark in Israel's history of this mortal collision between the prophets of two different and antagonistic gods.

This swift historical survey can be summarized as follows. In early Israel, *Yahweh* was known as God's name—but alongside many other names and divine appearances, and one must imagine a long period when the Yahweh faith was practiced side by side with Canaanite religion. Only with the Deuteronomistic theology does there appear to be a clear, determined, and programmatic separation.[13] Whether this then permits one to think of monotheism in Israel before Deuteronomy is the question. Bernard Land dryly observes of Gerhard von Rad's bold and pious claim—"a Yahweh-cult without the first commandment cannot really be imagined"—that although it is worthy of Karl Barth, the question is whether it is a historical judgment.[14] That a merging of titles, names, and concepts took place at least by the early monarchy can, however, be claimed by even the most demanding critical scholarship.[15] Names for God could be traded and passed across religious lines; Psalm 91 affords a striking example: "The one who dwells in the safe hiding-place of *Elyon*, who 'lodges overnight' in the shadow of *Shaddai*, is one saying to *Yahweh*, 'My refuge and my fortress; my *Elohim*, in whom I trust.' " Across religious lines and cultural situations some functions of deities remain essentially the same. Care and safekeeping feel the same, in general; the question is, Who is doing it? The dispute was not, Does it rain? or, Does deity bring rain? but, Who makes it rain? So, through years, even centuries, Israel lived with what cannot, strictly speaking, be called monotheism, polytheism, or even perhaps henotheism. What one sees is, rather, a mobile, changing process of accommodation and alteration taking place between conflicting religious and social forces, with varieties of opinions that may not always have been sharply defined. So, while someone says that Israel's faith was "more self-consciously monotheistic" around the time of Jeremiah,[16] another points out that Jeremiah still complained (Jer. 2:28; 11:13) that "your gods are as many as your cities, O Judah."[17] It was a slowly moving process by which over centuries there emerged the ultimately dominant idea that Yahweh alone is God. One cannot be sure when this idea became widely accepted; it is clearly stated in Hosea (cf. Hos. 2:16-20; 13:4).[18] Probably wide acceptance occurred within a gradual social movement; Martin Noth observed that persons' names compounded with "Yahweh" are found more frequently at the end of the monarchy,[19] and Hermann Vorländer expresses the common suspicion that Yahweh was worshiped more in the court, by the royal house, than by the people.[20] Even the acceleration of social and theological development brought about by the fall of Jerusalem and Judah, around which are associated all the forces for monotheism that were active behind Jeremiah, Ezekiel, Deutero-Isaiah, and the Deuteronomists, is actually a phenomenon spread over a period of a hundred years and part of a gradual process through which Israel's monotheism achieved definition.

Meanings and Associations Attached to the Name Yahweh

The meaning of the name Yahweh has been ardently and exhaustingly debated for years, and that debate will not be rehearsed here. There are questions in the debate that are of course very important: the degree to which the name is dependent upon the verb HYH/HYY,[21] where the name Yahweh might have originated (partial forms of the name occur in Ebla, Ugarit, Mari, and even, it is claimed, in Egypt), from where (if from anywhere else) Israel might have borrowed the worship of Yahweh, and the "true"—but stubbornly elusive—meaning of God's self-revelation in Exod. 3:14. But more important still is whether and to what degree these questions affected what any of the Old Testament traditions had in mind when the name Yahweh was used. One significant claim, for example, is that—whatever else "Yahweh" might have connoted—it meant "the one who is with you" (Exod. 3:12, "I AM with you").[22]

Surely the name Yahweh also meant more than that, but exactly what that was remains to be seen in the terms that qualified the word "Yahweh," or expressed Yahweh's being or action, or described Yahweh's qualities and forces.[23] Even if the meaning of the name Yahweh "had fallen into oblivion (except in priestly circles . . .) already very early," as A. Murtonen supposed,[24] the significance that remained would have been carried on through all the things that were said about Yahweh over the years.

Probably the most common term that adjectivally qualified Yahweh is "hosts" (*Sebaoth*). Occurring some 485 times, *saba* and its plural form are used to mean such different things as a host of armed forces, for war; the host of heaven (part of a celestial court? planetary and astral bodies?); common hard servant's work; and the undefined host around God. It is commonly found in a variety of combinations not only with Yahweh but also with Elohim and Adonai, and in more complicated phrases, a most descriptive one of which is in 1 Sam. 17:45, "Yahweh Sabaoth, Elohim of the ranks [armies] of Israel." This very important text points to one of the most common ways in the Old Testament to speak of God: Yahweh was a "man of war" (*'iš milhamah*, Exod. 15:3). God was addressed not only as the comforter and carer of Israel but also as the one who went to battle with Israel's armies. Simply tracing this quality in God's nature to the common ancient Near Eastern phenomenon of warrior gods only encourages one to avoid the fact that the Old Testament saw the making and the making-to-cease of wars as God's business, and took one of God's traits to be dependability and effectiveness in war. Yahweh Sebaoth was therefore also a term probably extending from Israel's very early days, from what for decades has been described as the Holy War traditions. But the terms Yahweh Sebaoth and Elohim of Sebaoth are not found in large tracts of the Old Testament, most notably the Hexateuch, and are instead very popular in the prophetic literature, especially in Isaiah of Jerusalem, Jeremiah, Haggai, Zechariah, and Malachi.[25] This may suggest that the term had something special to do with the cult in the Jerusalem temple traditions. In any case, God's warrior traits were not mere antiquarian habits, and from this and other evidence (cf. Lamentations) we know them to be vital and well known in the later Old Testament.

Another and even more common term attached to Yahweh was *Adon* ("lord"). This simple word, used of human sovereigns (e.g., in the Amarna letters) and found in a Canaaite name like Adoni-zedeq (Josh.

10:1) and at Ugarit, expressed a dominant conviction of faith about Yahweh.[26] Used frequently by Amos and Ezekiel in the title "Lord Yahweh," it was a primary linguistic pointer to what today is called a hierarchical view of God, namely, that God is Lord, dominating people and creation, ideally being served by them. Adon is, as it were, a benchmark against egalitarianism in the Old Testament's view of God.

This tenor in speaking of God can also be pursued elsewhere, through other terms. Lorenzo Vigano's summary in 1975 offers a useful handle on the subject. In addition to being called God, and Lord, Yahweh was thought of (Vigano would say, addressed) by such terms as Most High, Great One (me'od), Victor, and Terrible One. This chain of terms must be understood in connection with the theophanies of the Old Testament, a special genre of literature and theology. Theophanies made a particularly influential statement about how God was to be conceived and spoken of by Israel. Theophanies were no church picnic! The appearance of God was not just awesome; it was blinding, overwhelming, frightening, full of light and lightning, and terrible in imagery.[27] Facing God would be an awful, as well as awe-full, proposition (Amos 4:13). The "still small voice" imagery of 1 Kings 19 is without parallel elsewhere in the Old Testament, as Jörg Jeremias says.[28] Theophany occurs, rather, in cultic appearance or presentation of the divine king in a rousing and dramatic spectacle, and in cataclysmic disturbances of nature!

Other Associations in the Conception of God

On the other hand, God is known in the Old Testament through quite different qualities and through contrasting experiences. Yahweh was knowable as shepherd, calmly and skillfully caring for his fragile flock. Yahweh was faithful, gentle, deeply caring, loving, emotionally involved, and showing warm compassion to those who fear him. He was long of patience and generous in steadfast love and mercy (Ps. 103:8); he knows our nature and remembers that we are dust (Ps. 103:14). Vigano includes among his selections some terms that are comparable to this vein of thought, such titles as Preexistent, Eternal, Perennial, Just, Righteous, Guide, the Good One (or, Friend), the Neighbor, Wise One, and Ancient One. Psalm 136:1 says plainly, "Give thanks to Yahweh, for [he is] good!" God was not only terrible; God was good and gentle. "He does not always accuse; he doesn't stay angry forever! . . . As a father feels warm compassion for the children, so Yahweh feels warm compassion for those who fear [worship?] him" (Ps. 103.9, 13). The legendary gentleness of Yahweh, however, never more graphically expressed than in these words: "Like a shepherd he will pasture his flock; in his arm he will gather the lambs, and in his bosom he will carry them; he will lead the nursing ewes" (Isa. 40:11), was tenderly described in the context of the terrible, grisly fall of Jerusalem only a matter of decades before. On the divine-gentleness spectrum, the yin and the yang are never resolved in the Old Testament.[29]

In another category of God-language there are all those major theological attributes or qualities which may or may not be directly reflected in human experience. Hans-Joachim Kraus calls them the *proprietates Dei*, the perfections (and not the distinctive features) or Yahweh. To demonstrate these proper traits of God, he clusters together holy, glory, righteousness, steadfast love, and faithfulness.[30] One might easily add a second tier of terms as well, words for compassion, election, love, power, and so on. These qualities occupy a special place in the phenomenology of revelation and of God's being. They are not unrelated to human experience or to natural observation, but they do not directly emerge from that experience or observation. They are in a way sovereign over experience; they are the apodictic confessions of worship, the claims that sometimes fly in the face of experience and contradict it (cf., e.g., Psalm 44).

After scanning the Old Testament for ideas and for terms in thought and language about God, after all the naming and describing and recounting, one comes to realize that most terms and expressions derive from human experience and from nature. God is creator, shaper, shepherd, savior, redeemer, king, judge; God is like an enemy, like pus, rottenness, a lion. God is a shield, a horn of salvation, a rock, a refuge. God is a healer.[31] Through each of these words one senses the throb and pulse of human feeling and experience and sees the shape of natural phenomena. A delightful freedom empowered Old Testament speakers and authors to talk about the God of the terrible theophanies in homely social terms or with images from nature all around. The quantity and variety of simple images describing God illustrate the natural easiness and authenticity of God-language. Picturing God in terms of tending sheep, building a house, shattering and destroying vines and trees, shaking mountains, exploding in volcanos and in lightning, making grass grow, and healing all diseases—the Old Testament smoothly portrays God by using the categories and conditions of daily experience in its day, in the terms of science and knowledge in that "prescientific" age. God was the architect and the contract builder, not only in the world view but also in the universe view. God's was the law of gravity, the patterns of cause and effect. God "made die and made live" (1 Sam. 2:6). The Old Testament came to terms with God in the gentlest and in the cruelest expressions of nature and of human experience.

Another conclusion to distill from all these data is that the names for God did not carry all, or even the major share, of the theological freight. Even the name Yahweh, for all its majesty, in and of itself might be considered to be a rather flat concept. The contours, the texture, even to a large extent the structure, of conceptualizing God depended on the qualifying language, on what God did and how God was perceived (revealed) as doing it. Through that qualifying language Israel's theologians received revelation and reflected it on to the world. Oskar Grether[32] put all this contouring and texturing under the rubric of "Word" of God. Certainly creation by fiat ("by the word of Yahweh the heavens were made," Ps. 33:6), management and guidance of sociopolitical history by word (especially the prophetic word; cf. the Deuteronomistic History), and instruction for life and living through the words of Torah are all powerful evidence for Grether's classification. As a theological strategy Grether structured human experience and nature under the heading of Word and thus in effect set the stage for a doctrine of revelation which through that Word was applicable in a general as well as in a special way.

Two Special Issues

As one ponders how Israel conceived of and found names for God, two special issues call for attention. The first one permeates the entire Hebrew Scripture and its theology, lying always not far below the surface when it is not in fact the visible issue of the moment. We do not know whether the second was an issue in ancient Israel, but today it is a matter of pervasive concern for us, also just below the surface whenever it is not in fact patently clear.

Surging challengingly, sometimes it seems almost defiantly, through the theology of the Old Testament is that quality in God which can be called hiddenness, or unbeholdability. It is in many ways related to what Paul Volz called "das Dämonische in Jahwe." It was common experience among saints in Israel that God seemed to be alien, incomprehensible, and even unaccountable (cf. Job 9:32). God's presence was not only elusive[33] but also reclusive. God hides, in the experience of the chosen people. "Verily, you are El who is hiding himself, O Elohim of Israel, O

Savior" (Isa. 45:15), the prophet cries. God's response does not deny it: "In overflowing wrath I hid my face for a moment from you" (Isa. 54:8a). In the very era and tradition when God's power was most acclaimed and monotheism was argued in the strongest terms, the hiddenness of God was most plainly affirmed. Is there no connection between these facts? When God's oneness and uniqueness are most vigorously asserted, and the possibility of any other god utterly denied, must one not also have to leave a place for God's secretness?

The hiding of God no doubt referred to the experience of the fall of Jerusalem in 587 B.C.E. "For a brief moment I forsook you," God says (Isa. 54:7a), "like a wife of youth as she is rejected" (54:6b), but now "with everlasting *hesed* (steadfast love) I will have warm compassion on you, says Yahweh your Redeemer" (54:8b). The hiddenness is not made instrumental to the renewal of mercy; Israel is not urged to understand it as a necessary if unpleasant part of God's grand plan of salvation or deliverance of the people, and it is not offered as a painful but unavoidable link in a salvation's cause-and-effect chain. All this is remarkable because precisely after the fall one might have expected to find such a theological explanation here; it would have been so easy to satisfy Israel by making it clear that God was hidden because of Israel's sin or because of some greater good planned for the future.

Samuel Ballentine has put the question of God's hiddenness to a comprehensive study.[34] In dealing with the efforts to explain God's hiddenness as punishment, and as an expression of God's anger rather than arbitrariness, he follows the line of argument that sees in Israel's laments a way to cope with (N.B.: not resolve, or explain) God's hiddenness.

> In contrast to the prophetic literature, where Israel's response to this problem is obscured by an emphasis on divine punishment, and in contrast to the wisdom literature where the response is based on a calculated system of observation the success of which is limited by human capabilities, the psalms of lament place the emphasis on Israel's response as it was expressed in the cult. In this context the lament provides a form that serves both to enhance the articulation of the experience of the hiddenness of God and to limit the experience so that despair does not exceed the threshold of tolerance.[35]

At the end of his study Ballentine is thinking in positive, optimistic terms, expecting ways in which we may better understand God's hiddenness. That expectation is up to anyone to pursue, of course, and we today no doubt have the cultural conditioning and mentality to attempt to accomplish it. But the Old Testament left the question open, after some mighty wrestling. "Hiding the face" was a way of describing metaphorically, and perhaps humanly speaking, what it felt like to experience God's abandonment, wrath, inscrutable withdrawal, or failure to respond or answer. It was Israel's way of saying "I don't know" to questions about why God did or did not do this and that, why enemies and harmful forces had opportunity to hurt and to destroy.

God's hiddenness was clearly more than a matter of withholding visual perception because human beings should not see God and live. It was an indispensable part of a whole model for thinking about God and relating to God. Ballentine observes that the ideas of God's hiding his face, of forgetting, rejecting, and spurning, occur less frequently in the later Old Testament.[36] One may be permitted to ask: Was that because situations changed, or theology matured, or assumptions became bolder and more aggressive (or less aggressive, and less reckless)?

The second issue is a social one, demanded by questions raised in our own generation. Throughout this study the social process in Israel has been under observation; it is impossible to describe the history of God's names without taking that process into account. Social assumptions played important roles in naming God, and they provide some of the most intriguingly illusionary and frustratingly complex data in the investigation.

God is called king throughout the Old Testament, and there can be no doubt that in ancient Israel this was a dominant form in which the people thought of God. In the temple liturgy, major parts of the cultic action centered around God's reign, God's role as king, and God's relationship to the human kings of other nations. Individual and community hopes were fused into the acclamation of kingship; God's promise itself was a king's promise, regal and arbitrary, binding and grace-full. However despicable, lamentable, oppressive, or outrageous may have been the current monarch on the throne, the people and their worship institutions continued to call God their "king." If that was used as a manipulative, cynical means of social control by some malignant system, we'll probably never know. We should, however, beware of rash and unwarranted assumptions and not refuse to believe that ancient Israelites could think of God's kingship as a kind, secure, and good thing. Current efforts to find countervailing evidence against the old hierarchical assumptions can be applauded as a proper academic endeavor and may evoke our sympathetic support, but they are less than helpful if they warp the general shape of the evidence or attempt to deny the society in which the evidence is found.

God is also called father in the Old Testament—not often, but plainly and in several places.[37] God is never called mother.[38] God's work is compared to that of a parent, mother or father, or both.[39] This is the score card, if one is keeping a tally on the subject. The real issue is that Israel's God was certainly never thought to be a sexed being. The Old Testament does not say that God was not male; that would doubtless have struck Israelites as a ridiculous thing to say. The selected texts that have been applied to show that this claim was indeed made have been adequately dealt with by John Miller.[40] But surely the language used for God through the masculine pronouns was a symptom of much deeper issues and of social understanding and conventions that we deplore in our society.

The social meaning for *"father"* in Israel had to do with authority, care discipline, protection, and dignity.[41] It represented a role in a society that is harshly judged and incompletely understood today. It makes no sense to wish that Israel's God might not have been called father or king. At least, when God's work is compared to that of a parent, the language is warm, gentle, affectionate, nurturing, caring, and at the very least and by any account respectful. When God is called father the texts are talking about creation, leading, and affection. "Father" was a social assumption, part of the social and cultural mold into which the faith of the Old Testament was poured. Like "king," it had a rightful and necessary place in that mold; to remove it is not an editor's job, because it would require an operation with an incision three thousand years deep.

Conclusion

Can one discern a pattern, or any principles, in all of this Old Testament vocabulary about God? Did Israel, or did Old Testament authors, exercise any criteria for forming, utilizing, and keeping God-talk? Are there any criteria besides the name factor in identification and rejection (e.g., Baal, and "gods of the nations" were identified, to be rejected)? How can this discussion be summarized?

The fact is that there are no Old Testament guidelines for further summarizing these thoughts, for condensing a condensation. There is no authoritative, comprehensive list of such divine roles; to produce such a list would be to write a Cliff's Notes of the Bible. But, while never listed or specified, these roles do emerge from the texts to form a theological core. They have value comparable to the concepts of perfection singled out by Kraus to describe Yahweh. Isolated by themselves they seem barren. It is in the sacred texts that they function freely and surprisingly, doing what the word does (Isa. 55:11), illuminating and fleshing out the names of God, so that each generation hears for itself the language of God and perceives before it responsible ways to answer.

6

Edgar M. Krentz

GOD IN THE
NEW TESTAMENT

*T*he first century was a religious age.[1] "The sky hung low those
days." Human life was bounded and surrounded by gods of many
stripes. Every aspect of nature and life was related in some manner to its
correlative god.[2] Balbus, the Stoic philosopher in Cicero's *De natura deorum*, argues learnedly that the sun, the moon, and the five planets show
the intelligence, reason, and design inherent in the universe.[3] From these
characteristics Balbus, in good Stoic fashion, infers a "multitude of gods"
who give blessings to mortals. He names many of them. Augustine dealt
with this Roman attitude in defending Christians against the charge that
they caused the altars of the gods to be deserted and thus were responsible for the sack of Rome. He detailed the immorality of the Roman
gods[4] and rang the changes on the incongruities in the theology of Varro.
Augustine also drew on the critique of urban and civil theology in L. An-
naeus Seneca's *De superstitione*.[5]

God and the Gods

Christian commitment or a "modern scientific attitude" should not
obscure this pervasive religious dimension of ancient life. Gods there
were, of both sexes, in number great. They provided models and warrants for almost every type of activity. The licentious life style of Zeus and
Aphrodite (Jupiter and Venus, to give them their Roman names) was
more than balanced by the virtues of their spouses Hera and Hephaistos
(Juno and Vulcan). There was authentic piety, as the devotion of Aelius
Aristides to the healer Asclepius,[6] the description of Lucius's tie to Isis,[7]
the hymns to many deities and the aretalogies to Isis,[8] and the growth of

Dionysian worship[9] make evident. A similar case could be made for the worship of Aphrodite, the Syrian goddess, and for the prevalence of religious magic, divination, oracles, and the like. In this plethora of deities there is no evidence that women restricted their devotion to female deities and men to male deities. The "biological" gender of gods made little difference to their worshipers.

Twentieth-century people easily fall into the trap of thinking of these gods as mythological—that is, not having reality, or reflecting mere superstition—and retroject the attitude on to ancient people. That is a serious mistake and underestimates the significance of religion in the Roman era. Robert M. Ogilvie[10] will help one recover some empathy with the religions feeling of Romans in the first century.

Corinth is a good case study, since literature and archaeology have illuminated its history and character. Destroyed by the Romans in 146 B.C.E. and refounded as a Roman colony by Julius Caesar in 44 B.C.E., the surviving remains illustrate the richly variegated character of religion in the first century C.E.[11] The temple to Apollo dominates the agora (forum). Another temple overlooking the agora is dedicated to Roma. Temples and sacred precincts to Hera, Aphrodite, Asklepios, Demeter and Kore, Isis and Osiris, and Tyche stand out among many temples. The spring Peirene, sacred to Pegasus and Bellerophon, lay on Acrocorinth, along with a temple to Aphrodite. The biennial national games at the Isthmia were dedicated to Palaemon, whose temple has been excavated, while the port city Cenchreae had a notable temple to Isis. A lintel block inscribed "Synagogue of the Hebrews" and a console with three menoroth in the site museum testify to the presence of Judaism. These deities with their sacred precincts and cultic practices provided models for the nascent Christian communities. Cultic meals in cultic dining rooms (1 Corinthians 8–10) are illuminated by dining facilities at Corinthian temples.[12] Prophets and prophetesses, maenads and dervishes, cultic leaders and mystagogues were all present in the religions at Corinth. Given the pervasive climate of religion(s) at Corinth, significant influence on the language and practice of the Corinthian church is not surprising.

The New Testament reaction, however, is surprising to people of today. There is almost no polemic against the gods. In Acts 17:22, Paul praises the Athenians for their intense religious devotion ("I see that you are most religious in every respect"). There is no sarcasm in Paul's use of the word *deisidaimōn*, which I translated "most religious." Rather, the religious sensibilities of the Athenians are made the point of departure for the proclamation of Jesus and the resurrection. In 1 Cor. 8:4-6, Paul reacts to the many gods of Corinth. On the one hand, he cites the Corinthian claim, made in the light of the confession "There is no God but one," that "There is no image (*eidōlon*) in the cosmos" (8:4),[13] only to balance it by conceding the existence of "many gods and many lords" (8:5). To deny the existence of the many gods is to risk underestimating the danger in their cult. Over against these many gods and lords, however, Paul cites the credo

> But for us there is "one God, the Father,"
>> from whom are all things and unto whom we exist,
> and "one Lord, Jesus Christ,"
>> through whom all things are and through whom we exist (8:6).

God, identified as "the Father," is the source and goal of creation; the one Lord, Jesus Christ, is God's agent in creating the universe and the Corinthian Christian community. Paul separates God as Father from the many gods by his unique creative activity and Jesus from the many lords by his role in the creation.[14] The many gods are only *daimonia*, "godlets," as Paul calls them in 1 Cor. 10:20, scarcely to be named in the same rank as the one God, yet a danger to community with the Lord. One cannot sit at table with a "godlet," for example, Asklepios in his cult center, and also with Jesus in the Lord's Supper. That would be to deny both God and Jesus their unique role in the universe.

In Romans 1, Paul criticizes people for worshiping creature rather than creator; that is idolatry. But he is also critical of the Jews for blaspheming the name of God by their sacking of non-Jewish temples (Rom. 2:22-23). The gods of the Greco-Roman world occupy a strangely ambiguous position in Paul. Their reality is not questioned; mistreating their temples brings the name of God into disrepute. Yet they are a threat to the worship of the one God, the living and authentic creator.

Paul's stress on God as the creator may have profoundly influenced early Christian worship in the non-Jewish world. There is no record in the New Testament of the worship of God in temples or other sacred places. God the Creator is worshiped in the world he created, be it in some person's (nonsacred) house (cf. the house churches known in the Pauline corpus) or by the service (*leitourgia*) carried on by a renewed mind in this present evil world (Rom. 12:1-2).

No Proper Name for God

In some respects the New Testament is surprisingly reticent in the language it uses for God. The Old Testament is rich in names and epithets for God (see the chapter by Wesley Fuerst in this volume). That richness is not found in the New Testament. Even more striking is the complete absence of the Old Testament proper name of God from the New Testament. Thus the New Testament does not simply continue Old Testament practice in speaking of God. There is, for all of the lines of continuity, a break in the tradition.

A number of factors played into this disjunction. One was the change in attitude among some Jews about the use of God's proper name, based on a severe reading of Exod. 20:7 ("You shall not take the name of the Lord your God in vain; for the Lord will not hold him guiltless who takes his name in vain"). "Yahweh" became a name that was not to be pronounced (an *onoma arrēton*). Josephus, for example, called God's name "the name of God that makes the hair of those who say it stand on end."[15] Josephus does not dare to say aloud the name that God gave to Moses at the burning bush, not even in performing cultic acts!

> He [Moses] also besought Him not to deny him the knowledge of His name, but, since he had been granted speech with Him and vision of Him, further to tell him how He should be addressed, so that, when sacrificing, he might invoke Him by name to be present and the sacred rites. Then God revealed to him His name, which ere then had not come to men's ears, and *of which I am forbidden to speak.*[16]

A Jewish *tabula devotionis*[17] found in the necropolis of ancient Adrumetum in Roman Africa is a love spell. Domitiana, the daughter of Candida, calls on the God of the Jews under a wide variety of titles and epithets. She wants the God of Abraham to compel a certain Urbanus, the son of Urbana, to fall in love with her and marry her. In her magical formula Domitiana twice describes the name of God, the first time as "the precious and fear-producing and great name" (ll. 3-4) and the second as "the holy name that is not pronounced (l. 20). Josephus and Domitiana both knew that the naming of God's own proper name is to be avoided, for it is a dreadful, awful, threatening name.

A similar attitude is implied at Qumran. *The Manual of Discipline* contains a series of regulations prescribing the proper punishment for infractions of community life. One regulation reads:

> If any man has uttered the [Most] Venerable Name even though frivolously, or as a result of shock or for any other reason whatever, while reading the Book or praying, he shall be dismissed and shall return to the Council of the Community no more.[18]

This is the oldest known injunction against pronouncing the Tetragrammaton while reading the Hebrew Scriptures aloud. It is surprising and may account for a scribal convention in this community. Qumran scribes wrote some biblical manuscripts in the paleo-Hebrew script, apparently a mark of their sanctity. They regularly wrote their sectarian, nonbiblical texts in the contemporary round script, using the archaic letter forms only for the divine name, for example, in 1QpHab and 1QH.[19] This practice was also followed in some Septuagint manuscripts,[20] a practice that Origen of Alexandria pointed out in his *Commentary to Ps. 2:2.*[21] The writing of the divine name in a "strange" script or alphabet called it to the attention of the reader and prevented him from pronouncing it aloud.

This rigid interpretation of the Second Commandment is explicit in post-Jamnia Judaism. "If a rabbi (who has authority to do so) hears a man using the name of heaven idly, he must excommunicate him, upon pain of a like sentence himself" (*Nedarim* 7b).[22] Years ago Gustav Dalman called attention to numerous "evasive or precautionary modes of referring to God"[23] used by Jews in the Mishnaic period. Pronouncing the divine name was avoided by the use of the "numinous passive," by referring to "the Name," "the Heavens," or "the Place." Many of these precautionary modes of God-reference are found in Matthew, for example, in his standard phrase "kingdom of the heavens" where Mark and Luke have "kingdom of God."

Jews observed the same practice in the worship of the synagogue. In the first-century synagogue, Jews prayed the first part of the Kaddish as they prepared to worship. God's name is not used:

> May His great name be magnified and hallowed in the world, which He has made according to His will, and may His kingly rule be established in your life time—in your time and in the time of the whole house of Israel. May the name of the Lord be praised from now on and forever. May the prayer and petition of all Israel find acceptance before our Father who is in heaven.[24]

And before the homily later in worship the second part of the Kaddish was prayed: "Upon Israel [and the rabbis and their scholars and those who learn from their scholars] and all who study the Law in this place and everywhere, may there be grace and mercy and compassion and deliverance from our Father who is in heaven." In both sections the phrase "our Father who is in heaven" serves as a reference to God that avoids the naming of the name.

The core petitions of the Shemoneh Esreh, the great prayer of the synagogue liturgy, antedate Jesus.[25] They use a rich arsenal of descriptive language to bless God and invoke his aid:

> 1. Blessed art thou, O Lord, God of Abraham, God of Isaac and God of Jacob, God most high, who art the possessor [creator] of heaven and earth, our Shield and the Shield of our fathers. Blessed art Thou, O Lord, the Shield of Abraham!
>
> 2. Thou art mighty, strong, that livest forever, that raisest the dead, that sustainest the living, that quickenest the dead. Blessed art Thou, O Lord, who quickenest the dead!
>
> 3. Holy art Thou and Thy Name is to be feared, and there is no God beside Thee. Blessed art Thou, O Lord, the holy God!
>
> 4. O favour us, our Father, with knowledge from Thyself and understanding and discernment from Thy torah. Blessed art Thou, O Lord, who vouchsafest knowledge!
>
> 5. Cause us to return, O Lord, unto Thee, and let us return anew (in repentance) in our days as in the former time. Blessed art Thou, O Lord, who delightest in repentance!
>
> 6. Forgive us, our Father, for we have sinned against Thee; blot out and cause our transgression to pass from before Thine eyes. Blessed art Thou, O Lord, who dost abundantly forgive!
>
> 7. Look upon our afflictions and plead our cause, and redeem us for the sake of Thy Name. Blessed art Thou, O Lord, the Redeemer of Israel!

The Tetragrammaton is avoided completely. In its place God's qualities or past actions to Israel are recalled. The New Testament follows this same linguistic pattern.

Language for God in the New Testament

The New Testament does not have the rich variety of language for God that characterizes much of the Old Testament. One fact noted earlier bears repeating: God's proper name does not appear in the New Testament. Nor do the writers of the New Testament borrow extensively from the language of Hellenistic Judaism. There is, for example, little use of the *via negativa* in describing God such as one finds in Josephus, *Against Apion* 2.167: "[Moses] revealed him as one, not born, for all time unchangeable, exceeding all mortal conception in beauty, on the one hand made known to us in power [or potentially], unknowable however as to what he is in his essence." James 1:17 comes closest when it applies language derived from solar phenomena to God "the Father of lights, with whom there is no change of position [i.e., no movement like the sun] and no diminution of light caused by the winter solstice." A survey of the linguistic data in the major writers of the New Testament will support the generalizations made above.

Paul

Paul usually says simply "God." "God" occurs 146 times in Romans, usually without modifiers. Paul does speak of "the God of endurance and comfort" (Rom. 15:5), of "the God of peace" (15:33; 16:20), and of "the God of hope" (15:13), all in liturgical formulae that he probably inherited from Judaism. His use of the phrase "the immortal God" (*ho aphthartos theos*, 1:23) probably comes to him from the Hellenistic Jewish apologetic tradition that underlies the argument of Romans 1, while the liturgical blessing of God (*berakah*), "who is God over all, blessed forever, Amen" (9:5) derives from Jewish piety (cf. the synagogue prayers above). The (Jewish) confession "God is one" occurs in Rom. 3:30 (cf. 1 Cor. 8:6; Gal. 3:20) as Paul argues that the unity of God demands that God be the God of all peoples. Thus, where Paul uses language that describes or expands the simple term "God," he is usually dependent on Jewish formulations that avoid the divine name.[26]

Paul also describes God as "the God who raises the dead and calls nonexistent things into existence" in Rom. 4:17. But that is scarcely a name; rather it is a description that stresses the creative power of God. The phrase "he who raised Jesus from the dead" (8:11) is similar. This provides the background for his use of the term "Father" for God as described below. There is a rich store of nouns associated with "God." These terms stress God's gospel (1:1), power (1:16), righteousness (1:17; cf. "God the justifying" in 8:33), grace (5:15), love, and so on. It is not surprising that Paul speaks of "the mercying God" (9:16, using a barbarous English translation to stress the participle in the Greek). There are also terms that stress the wrath (1:18) and judgment of God (cf. 9:22). None of them, however, serve as a name for God, though they provide a rich lode from which to mine a description of Paul's God.

Paul calls God "Father" a few times in Romans. Twice the term is used in association with "the Lord Jesus Christ": Rom. 1:7 greets with "Grace to you and peace from God our Father and from the Lord Jesus Christ." The last specific hortatory paragraph concludes by asking God to grant unity of mind in order that "with one accord with one mouth you might glorify the God and Father of our Lord Jesus Christ" (Rom. 15:6). This serves as the basis for the appeal to "receive [i.e., accept] one another as Christ also received you to the glory of God" (15:7). It was the glory of God that raised Jesus from the dead (6:4) and so impels us to newness of life. The reception of the Spirit enables the acclamation (note the verb "shout") to God 'Abba, the father" (Rom. 8:15; cf. Gal. 4:6-7) and that is the basis for our conviction that we are God's children. This pattern of God-related language found in Romans is repeated in the other Pauline letters with only minor variation.[27]

Ephesians

Ephesians, a later, deutero-Pauline document, reflects a somewhat different pattern in its terminology for God. It too uses the term "God" frequently, twenty-three times in the six chapters, though that is statistically less frequent than in Romans. One might argue that the frequent use of the emphatic pronoun "he" (*autos*) is an implicit use of the term "God" throughout the letter (fourteen occurrences in Ephesians 1 alone!). He is "the God of our Lord Jesus Christ, the Father of glory" (Eph. 1:17).

God is also the "Creator"; the management of the mystery hidden from the foundation of the world in the "God who created the universe" (*ta panta*) is now being revealed according to his purpose in Christ Jesus our Lord (Eph. 3:9-11). That language marks one significant change from Romans and the other Pauline letters: Ephesians stresses in an unprecedented fashion the cosmic dimension in its language about God. Stress falls on God's will (1:5, 11), wisdom (1:8; 3:10), plan (1:4; 3:11), glory (1:12; 14, 17 ["the Father of glory"]) and the "mystery" they stress. God's will is this eternal, mysterious plan (1:5, 9, 11; 3:9-11). God is the cosmic ruler whose will bends the course of history to his purpose and plan.

Ephesians differs from Romans in another manner: the term "Father" is used much more frequently. The opening berakah blesses "the God and Father of our Lord Jesus Christ who has blessed us" (1:3; cf. Col.

1:3). God is "the Father" to whom both Jew and non-Jew have access through Jesus (2:18). Thus the cosmic creator is the Father whom all people can now approach. The writer "bends his knees to the Father, from whom every family [or clan, *patria*] in heaven and on earth gets its name (3:14-19). Here God's fatherhood exists prior to the salvific action in Christ, and therefore is the basis of a true patronymic. In 4:6 the writer expands the Jewish credo ("One God") by adding "and Father of the universe (*pantōn*), he who is over all and through all and in all," an addition that softens the harsh overtones of the universally present creator. In the sevenfold unity only the one God as Father gets a descriptive epithet. Hymnody is to give thanksgiving "to our God and Father"[28] for everything in the authority (name) of our Lord Jesus Christ (5:20). The cosmic note is sounded again. God is also named Father in the concluding blessing (6:23). The term "Father" is much more significant in Ephesians than in authentic Paul.

Mark

What factors led to this marked difference between Paul's authentic letters and Ephesians? One enters the realm of speculation at this point. Ephesians probably was written sometime in the ninth decade of the first century, though a date in the tenth decade is possible.[29] Between Paul and Ephesians the Gospels emerge, and among them Matthew and John elevate the title "Father" to a new significance. Mark, the earliest Gospel, most frequently says simply "God" in absolute form or in combination with some other term. Thus Mark four times uses the title "Son of God" (Mark 1:1; 3:11; 5:7 ["Son of the most high God"]; 15:39), speaks of "the gospel of God" (1:14), "the house of God" (2:26), "the will of God" (3:35), "the word (*logos*) of God" (7:13), and "the royal rule of God" (thirteen times: 1:15; 4:11, 26, 30; 9:1; 10:14, 15, 23, 24, 25; 12:34; 14:25; 15:43). Twice he uses or implies the Jewish credo "God is one" (2:7; 10:18; cf. 12:32), and once (12:26) cites the self-identification "I am the God of Abraham, Isaac, and Jacob." Jewish periphrases also occur, though somewhat rarely. Mark speaks of "the Heavens" (1:1; 6:41; 8:11; 9:7; 11:30-31), "the Blessed" (14:61), and "the Power" (14:61), all periphrases for God.

Jesus is also related to God. The demons call him "the holy one of God" (1:24), while Jesus himself speaks of God as "he who sent me" (9:37). The term "Father" is used of God four times, in no consistent pattern. Twice Jesus refers to God as "Father" in eschatological contexts.

"The Son of Humanity will be ashamed of them, whenever he comes in the glory of his Father with the holy angels" (8:38); no one knows the time "of that day or hour," not the angels in heaven, nor the Son, but only the Father (13:32). These passages do not interpret the significance of God as Father. Two other passages suggest a bit more. Commenting on the withered fig tree, Jesus tells his disciples that they should forgive others when praying in order that "your Father who is in the heavens might forgive you your transgressions" (11:25). God as Father relates reciprocally to the disciples in forgiveness. The most important passage is Mark 14:36. Jesus in Gethsemane prays "Abba, Father, all things are possible for you," as preface to his request that the cup be removed. Yet he prays for the Father's will to be done. God the Father is he whose plan takes Jesus to the cross (cf. the "must" in 8:31). Mark 14:36 has had signal importance in discussing the historical Jesus' relationship to God as far surpassing "any possibilities of intimacy assumed in Judaism, introducing indeed something wholly new."[30]

Luke-Acts

The two-volume work Luke-Acts has a restricted repertoire of theo-referent language. Luke uses the term "God" 122 times in the Gospel and 168 times in Acts. (Some occurrences in the Gospel are in the phrase "royal rule of God.") The Gospel uses "Lord" (*kyrios*) of God eighteen to twenty-two times (depending on some judgment calls as to whether the referent is God or Jesus) and Acts thirteen times. Other terms are used of God. God is "the Powerful One" (Luke 1:49), "the despot" (Luke 2:29), "the Savior" (Luke 1:47), "the one who speaks to Moses" (Acts 7:44), and "the Most High" (Luke 1:32, 34, 76; 6:35; Acts 7:47). Twice Luke uses the term "the [my] Father" (2:49; 9:26 [Markan]) and thrice refers to "your Father" (6:36; 12:30, 32). He prayed in thanksgiving to God as "Father" (10:21), in intercession for himself (22:42) and others (22:34, 46) and taught his disciples to address God as Father in the Lord's Prayer (11:2). Finally, by virtue of his sonship to God he mediated knowledge of God (10:22) and promised a share in the eschatological rule of Israel (22:29). Jesus as son of the Father mediates access to the Father. Yet, one must recognize, the term "Father" does not dominate Lukan language about God.

Matthew

Matthew and John show important changes in the pattern of language for God. Matthew uses the term "God" fifty-one times, often in highly significant phrases. The crowds glorify "the God of Israel" (15:31) when they see the Isaianic deeds that Jesus does. Continuity with the promises of the past is stressed (cf. 11:2-6). Peter confesses Jesus as "the Anointed, the Son of the living God" in 16:16, while Jesus acknowledges that title when put under oath "by the living God" in 26:63. The phrase "the living God," an Old Testament oath formula,[31] lends majesty to the confession at Caesarea Philippi. The confession distinguishes Jesus as the "Son of God" from all "Divine Men" of the ancient world. Jesus is related to him who is the living God of Israel, the One by whom Israel lived and hoped. Jesus himself responds to that oath formula by affirming his unique role in God's plan.

Matthew has other striking phrases to call God to mind. God is "the One able to destroy life and body in Gehenna" (10:28), "the One who inhabits the temple" (23:21), "the One seated upon the throne of God" (23: 22), "the Great King" (5:35), "a luminous cloud" (17:5), "the heavens" (twenty-six times, most in the plural, twice in the singular), frequently used in the phrase "the royal rule of the heavens" as a substitute for God. Matthew makes more use of periphrases for God than do Mark and Luke, as these expressions suggest. "Lord" (kyrios) refers to God in at least thirteen passages. Jesus is also conscious of a special relationship to God, who is "he who sent me" (10:40).[32]

Matthew's striking and frequent use of "Father" for God marks his most significant departure from Markan and Lukan patterns. He uses the term over forty times in a variety of expressions. "[The] Father," either used absolutely or qualified by "your," occurs some fifteen times.[33] "The [my, your, our] Father who is in the heavens" [plural] occurs fifteen times.[34] "The [your] heavenly Father" occurs seven times (5:48; 6:14, 26; 32; 15:13; 18:35; 23:9),[35] while "Your Father who sees in secret" is named three times (6:4, 6, 18, also a phrase unique to Matthew in the New Testament) and "your Father, the One in secret" occurs in 6:6, 18. Disciples are to baptize "in the name of the Father, the Son and the Holy Spirit" (28:19). The Spirit of their Father speaks in the disciples (10:20). In the Christian community the title "Father" is to be reserved for God alone: "Do not call anyone 'Father' upon the earth, for One is your Father, the heavenly One" (23:9).[36] Father as address to God and title for God is a special characteristic of Matthean theology; it is used to describe God in relation to Jesus and the disciple community.

Robert Hamerton-Kelly points out that Matthew "presents the most vivid interpretation of the father idea" among the four Gospels.[37] He asserts that use of Father clusters in three key passages: the "catechesis on prayer" in Matt. 6:1-18,[38] a "catechesis on conduct in the church" in 18:10-35, and "advice on how to endure persecution" in 10:16-32. Matthew 6:1-18 details the conditions under which our petitions are received by God. "God is a Father who rewards the modest, hears those of few words, and forgives us when we are forgiving towards others." Matthew 18:10-35 is of a piece, though it applies to inner-community relationships. Father is used of God in worship and the communal life of the church. The Spirit of the Father, entering the believer, also enables confession in the face of persecution and so promotes the survival of the community. Matthew adds the term "Father" to many of the inherited Q sayings in these sections to make clear that disciples have the power and hope to live out of their experience of the forgiving Father they know in Jesus.

The Fourth Gospel

The Gospel of John refers to God in three main ways. "God" is used eighty-three times in John, a perfectly normal pattern.[39] "Father" is used 108 times to refer to God, in most instances to denote the special relationship of Jesus to God. Jesus also refers to God as "he who sent me" nineteen times. Beyond these three major modes of referring to God, John once uses the periphrasis "from the heavens" (12:28) and uses the term "Lord" in a few Old Testament citations.

At first this seems to be a somewhat impoverished mode of referring to God. But John achieves depth of thought by adding modifiers or predicatives to this language. God is the "one father" (8:41), "the only God" (*monos theos*, 5:44), the "truth" (3:33), "the only true God" (17:3; cf. 8:26). God is Jesus' "very own Father" (*idion patera*, 5:18), "the Father who sent him" (i.e., Jesus, 5:23; cf. 8:16, 18; 9:3-4), "the living Father" who is the cause of life in Jesus (6:57, applying to the Father an attribute of God in the Old Testament), who is "true" (8:26), the one "who is glorifying" Jesus (8:54). All who claim God as Father should love Jesus, since he "went out from the Father" (8:42). "God" is used only three times in the upper room discourse (16:27, 30; 17:3); these chapters are rich in "Father" language (twenty times in chap. 14, ten in chap. 15, ten in chap. 16, six in chap. 17). Finally, so to speak, Father is the primary mode of referring to God for the Johannine Jesus. He tells Mary that he is going up "to my Father and your Father, to my God and your God" (20:17). God is identified as the Father who sends Jesus as the revealer, the source of the paraclete, the glorified One who draws all people to himself.[40]

Other New Testament Writers

Later books of the New Testament show some acculturation to Hellenistic modes of referring to the divine. First Tim. 1:17 still uses the Jewish credo of the one God (1 Tim. 2:5, a credal formula), but also uses some typical Hellenistic epithets for God: "immortal, invisible, only wise God" (1 Tim. 1:17, much like the *via negativa* of Josephus; cf. Jude 4-25). The introduction to the hymnic passage in 1 Tim. 6:15-16, which describes God as the one "who alone has immortality," calls God "the blessed and sole dynast" (1 Tim. 6:15). Hebrews is, in this respect, surprisingly untouched by Hellenistic influence; the reference to God as "majesty in high places" (Heb. 1:3) is the closest it comes to Hellenistic language. Finally, the Apocalypse presents God in apocalyptic language as essentially uninvolved in history, yet overseeing the unrolling of the apocalyptic drama from the heavenly throne and acting through the lamb slaughtered from the foundation of the world (cf. Revelation 4–5, et passim).

James Reese did a statistical survey of modes of referring to God in the New Testament, reported in a short but important article.[41] He identified 421 usable pieces of data for reconstructing New Testament patterns. (Unfortunately, the article was too brief to include tables or listings of these data bits.) He claims that 183 (or 43 percent) of these data bits refer to God as "Father" absolutely, or as the Father of Jesus or the believer. Every document in the New Testament, except 3 John, uses this model at least once. It is clearly the dominant model. Sixty-five percent of the references in John and 56 percent of those in Matthew use this mode. Paul (excluding Ephesians and the Pastorals) uses it 15 percent of the time, Ephesians 25 percent. Elsewhere it is quite rare. The only other model used frequently, though not to the same degree, is what Reese calls "the God of Salvation History." It is especially prominent in Acts, Romans 9–11, and Luke 1–2. Cosmological interest is rare, as are abstract terms. Action words such as "living" and "powerful" are more frequent. Reese's summary reinforces what we have said above and suggests that the Father-language deserves special treatment.

God, Father of Jesus and the Disciple

In 1924 Karl Holl, the Berlin church historian, published an essay entitled "Urchristentum and Religionsgeschichte" in the journal *Zeitschrift für systematische Theologie*.[42] Holl asked what distinguished

Christianity from the religions about it in the first century, when it appeared to be just one more migrant Eastern cult. His answer was that Jesus' conception of God was unique. "Jesus preaches a God who wants to have dealing with sinful men, a God to whom he who has sunk deep stands, in certain circumstances, especially near" (Eng. trans., p.15). Holl held that this was not a romantic notion, for "Jesus . . . sees a deep gulf between God and man. According to Him salvation consists . . . in this, God of His free grace comes down to meet man" (p.17). This, claims Holl, was a new insight, even in Judaism, that prevented Christianity from being swallowed up in the syncretistic caldron holding the religious stew of the first century.

Eight years later (1932) Rudolf Bultmann published an essay titled "Urchristentum und Religionsgeschichte."[43] The identical title is intentional. Bultmann argued that Jesus was Jewish, remained Jewish, and had no new conception of God.[44] The two views are diametrically opposed. Bultmann apparently held to his view. His discussion of Jesus' message in his *New Testament Theology*[45] regards it as a "presupposition" for New Testament theology. The section on "Jesus' Idea of God" (22-26) places Jesus in the prophetic tradition but regards him as one who individualized (i.e., dehistoricized) God's demand and forgiveness. Jesus differs from Judaism in his idea of history but not in his view of God. The disjunction between Holl and Bultmann on this point was taken up in the resumption of the quest for the historical Jesus. His understanding of God remains an important issue.

It is a truism in New Testament studies today that Jesus called God by the Aramaic term *abba*.[46] The term occurs three times in the New Testament: Mark 14:36; Rom. 8:15; and Gal. 4:6. Only the first is on Jesus' lips. In each case the Greek translation "the father" *ho patēr* is immediately added. The term is infrequent in rabbinic literature,[47] while "Father" is often on Jesus' lips for God in the Gospels. In Gethsemane, Jesus expressed the conviction that his actions were the direct outcome of the will of God. *Abba* expressed closeness to God because it is an intimate familial term. Jesus lived in the conviction that the Father knew him, that he knew the Father, and that through him God as Father is close to the disciples and known by them as a God of mercy.[48] This unusual term survived in the church in Aramaic, even though it needed translation (Rom. 8:15; Gal. 4:6). The force of this tradition indicates that the term expressed something prized by the church. Many times "Father" in Jesus' words in Matthew is the result of later redaction. The term is inserted into new and fitting contexts because of what Jesus himself had done and taught.

Jesus proclaimed the nearness of God to save. He ate with publicans and sinners, the outcasts of society, and so established table fellowship with them. All Jewish meals began with a blessing of the name of God. Jesus affirmed the value of sinners to God by eating with them.[49] The table was also a place of prayer and praise, and therefore also of community. (When Ephesians begins with a berakah on God as Father, it continues Jesus' table practice and the customs of the synagogue.)

Jesus taught his disciples to pray to God as Father. The term "Father" is familial, that is, relational. Its function is not to stress God's sex, God's maleness, but God's close immediacy to Jesus and his disciples. They can address God in prayer, knowing that he responds. The Lord's Prayer, probably closest to its Jesuanic form in Luke 11:2-4, explicates what "Father" means by the content of the petitions. God hallows his name by vindicating himself through the gathering again of his people (cf. Ezekiel 36). God is called to rule as king, a message of comfort for his people (Isaiah 40); he will gather the scattered exiles and bring them to the land. The prayer for bread asks that God act in care for his people as he did in the exodus. "Father" is a term that expresses faith in God as one who keeps his covenant promises.

Romans extends Jesus' own language by relating the fatherhood of God to the resurrection of Jesus. "Christ was raised from the dead by the glory of the Father" (Rom. 6:4).[50] The resurrection of Jesus shows that God is indeed God, who calls nonexistent things into existence, who makes the dead alive (Rom. 4:17, 24). The resurrection of Jesus manifests the fatherhood of God and so calls for faith in the God who justifies the ungodly. It is the ultimate proof that God is the creator who enlivens the baptized by the gift of the Spirit. The Spirit produces adoption into the family of God, and so we shout the acclamation "*Abba*, the Father" (Rom. 8:15). The new relationship is correlated with new action, new acceptance, new thinking that makes new community and so glorifies the God and Father of our Lord Jesus Christ. Romans 12–15 culminates in 15:5-6 and leads to the command, "Therefore receive one another, just as Christ received you to the glory of God."[51]

Ephesians closes the circle in many ways. The sevenfold "one" in Eph. 4:4-5 ties the triple christological and ecclesial acclamation "one Lord, one faith, one baptism" to the confession of the "one God, the creator Father, who is over all and through all and in all" because it is through Christ that God "fills all things in everyone" (Eph. 1:23). Creation and Christology have met together, the Father and the Son kissed each other in this creed. Thereby the term "Father" for God is firmly anchored in a soteriological center. "Father" describes the relationship of salvation to God, effected by the Son, in which we have access to the Father and so live in hope.

Conclusion

No term or name does justice to all that God, Jesus, or the Spirit is (are). Titles in variety reveal glimpses of the reality that God is. Problems arise when biblical names or titles are replaced by functional terms that tend to be abstractions. Leander Keck, discussing Christology, says:

> There would be no christology if there were no soteriology because it is what Christians claim about Jesus as the bringer or effector of salvation that generates the question of his identity. To oversimplify: soteriology makes christology necessary; christology makes soteriology possible. To paraphrase: Jesus' significance must be grounded adequately in his identity. At the same time christology is not reducible to soteriology because, at least in the classical Christian tradition, Christ is always more than Saviour.[52]

The same principle applies to our theology. God is to be correlated with soteriology. Soteriology clarifies who God is, and who God is is expressed in soteriology. Remove the soteriological center and the doctrine of God is abstract and threatening. To know God as the Father of Jesus is to know him as merciful and forgiving.

Keck adds in footnote 6: "It should not be overlooked that the formula 'Creator, Redeemer and Sustainer,' which is now being substituted, in some Anglo-Saxon quarters, for 'Father, Son and Holy Spirit,' not only replaces a Trinity of Persons with a triadic functionalism but also constricts the role of the Second Person to redemption—a move which lacks clear warrant in the NT." Keck's argument is clear and convincing. To depersonalize God or Jesus is to change the biblical God into a theological or philosophical abstraction. Not only does that confine the work of God to specific persons in the Trinity (i.e., deny the old principle that *opera ad extra indivisa sunt*), it also destroys the pattern of relationships that underlies the Christian's relationship to God through Christ.

7   Robert W. Bertram

PUTTING THE NATURE OF GOD INTO LANGUAGE: NAMING THE TRINITY

*N*othing so defies "putting the nature of God into language" as does God's triunity, except that even that much languaging is already prompted by the nature of God. In the creeds certainly that is what occasions the triune language: not merely the *experience* of God—so far Friedrich Schleiermacher was right, "religious consciousness" alone would never yield the credal trinity[1]—but *Godself*. That is admittedly a God experienced, yet God "in person." Of course, the triune God whom Christians experience may not be God *"per se,"* "by himself" (Schleiermacher's caricature), in disincarnate isolation. Their God is always "God in Christ," *per Christum*. God is experienced as theirs—God *pro nobis*, "our God"—in the Word about Jesus, which itself comes through Spirited language. Still, that triune God, as Christians trust even in the face of God's nontriune, devastating appearances to the contrary, *deus absconditus*, is nevertheless truly God. The triune God in Christ through the Spirit, God relating to us, need not be God *per se* in order to be God *in se*, God indeed.[2]

God the Child

What is that primal Worded experience which at bottom occasions all language about God as triune? Is it not the experience of being reconciled to God in Jesus the "Son," indeed to God *as* Jesus the Son? "The entire apostolic confession of faith is contained in these words, 'You are Christ, the Son of the living God.' "[3] Even if the reference to Jesus as

"Son," in which the New Testament abounds, is in some cases interpo-
lation and not original or is a later development of "Word" or "Wisdom,"
it is as basic to the faith and especially to its trinitarian formulation as are
the references to Jesus as "Lord" and "Christ."[4]

It is this primal filial reference—filial not male—in the trinitarian
identification of Jesus on which I wish to dwell, not first the mathemati-
cal mystery of three-yet-one but first the scandalous joy that the one God
on whom everything depends is simultaneously as we are, one who depends—a child! But the Child is not for that reason any less God. On the
contrary, that also is of the essence of God: not only to be depended
upon as a parent but also, as an offspring ("begotten"), to depend for
very life and being upon the parent. The one who is depended upon is of
course God, but the one who does the depending is likewise God, the
selfsame God. The latter assertion is as important as the former.

From the former assertion, that it is God who is depended upon, it
should be clear that we are not now—not yet!—speaking about God's
depending upon the *world*, not even upon the worldly man Jesus or
upon the worldly proclamation of his gospel or upon worldly people's
believing it. That comes later. The Trinity is also a biography, a career,
whose story must be told in sequence. Nor are we talking, either now or
later, about Alfred North Whitehead's God whose "consequent nature"
depends for its "enrichment" on the temporal world process—not if that
bypasses God's prior depending, as Son, upon Godself.[5] For now, in the
priorities of the Trinity, what is being depended upon by God the Child
is the "one God, the Father, the almighty." In other words, I would like to
renew Arianism's reminder that the Son is subordinate to the Father but,
rather than argue from this to subordinationism, affirm with orthodoxy
that the Son is Godself not in spite of but because of this dependent (not
creaturely) status.

For is it not equally important to the faith that the dependent too is
God? And God is dependent not first in the incarnation where simply as
the man Jesus he might have qualified as one of the "children of God"
the way his human followers now do. Presupposed in his incarnation,
prior to it, is that he has been not just the child of God as others are but
uniquely *God* the Child. Notice, here God's dependence upon God is not
like some solitary individual's self-enclosed reliance upon oneself, solo,
but is rather like one person's reliance upon another, vis-à-vis. That "distinction of persons" is no doubt occasioned by Jesus the Christ's vis-à-vis
relation to his Father while on earth. Yet it must be enormously impor-

tant to the Christian faith that that same Child-to-Parent relationship be asserted right within the deity, preincarnation, in spite of all the pains which that then requires in order to remain utterly monotheistic. For why else is it that not the Father or the Spirit becomes (and forever remains) incarnate but only the Son does? Nor is it with the Father or with the Spirit that believers are identified as siblings, as junior deities, but only with the Son.

The Problem

My laying such instant stress on the second member of the Trinity to the relative exclusion of the first member, not to mention the third (both these imbalances will be redressed later), and above all my stressing the second member's sonship, his childhood, his dependence, is deliberate. It is intended to right a wrong. The wrong in this case is the widespread aversion to conceiving of dependence as divine. Conversely, it is the widespread fixation upon deity exclusively as autonomy or sovereignty—always loving, of course, maybe even vulnerably loving, yet finally underived, unbeholden, unsubmissive, unaccountable, and in that respect unlike us. Joan Chamberlain Engelsmann faults what she call's "Philo's law of preeminence": "Anything feminine cannot be divine and anything divine must be masculine." Another, at least as sinister "preeminence" which usually goes unnoticed altogether is that anything filial cannot be divine and anything divine must be parental.[6]

We are all aware of the natural antitrinitarian prejudice, even among trinitarians, that of the three "persons" it is only the Father who is properly God, or the slightly more sophisticated prejudice which does not really need three "persons" at all so long as one, parental God manages to create, redeem, and sanctify. My present concern, however, is not only with the transparent modalism in this prejudice but with its antipathy to God's being "begotten," an offspring, God's being (so to speak) on the receiving end, as God the Son is and is all the while "very God." Here the question is not, Might God be a mother? but rather (as Nestorius asked in disbelief), Might God *have* a mother—a human one, at that—as we do?

This brings to mind the example (though there are others equally current) of the present debate about gender in God-talk. Specifically, notice the preoccupation with God the Parent, whether as "Father" or "Mother" or both. Often the controversy over God as "Father," which by itself is wholesome and long overdue, conceals an underlying consensus among the most diverse antagonists which is not wholesome, and that is their at least tacit assumption that nothing so defines deity as does its parent-like power, the power to be depended upon or, more invidiously, the power to command respect and to obligate and ingratiate. Given that narrow prejudgment about what is most godlike about God, theological energies are then spent over whether divine power so exclusively conceived is more paternal or maternal, more muscular or nurturing, but of course both, all the while reinforcing the theistic though unchristian assumption that all that counts is that God is parental.

Once that parentalist preclusiveness is allowed to exhaust the divine dignity it is no wonder that patriarchalists cling to paternal designations of God and that feminists (including myself) contest their monopoly. The danger is that both camps might proceed from the same parentalist myopia. The impression sometimes given is that it is the first member of the Trinity, the one on whom everything depends, who alone holds the key to world control, and so the naming of that first "person" must reflect also the political aspirations of human beings who seek to retain or to wrest control. Nothing so vividly illustrates that ideology as does patriarchalism. The feminist protest will have to be free enough not to fall into the same trap, thus internalizing the oppressor. I am not proposing that the time has come for children to organize themselves into theological filialists, though they might have a point. But no need, the Trinity has anticipated that point.

A Bad Name

Amid the concern over the naming of God the Father, what may easily be overlooked is that it is no less the Son who has gotten a bad name, and not only because of that name's maleness but especially because of its childness. Sons, like daughters, are derivative, dependents, and it is dependence that has gotten a bad name. Maybe patriarchalism is to be blamed for that casualty, too, though I doubt that is the whole of it. And though theological feminism may not be the rescue operation that promises to rediscover the gospel's liberated, creative sort of dependence—but then again maybe it is—it has, I believe, along with other versions of liberationism exposed how cruelly dependence can be demonized. That discovery has advanced the whole question of theological naming, beyond metaphysical questions about finite names for infinite realities to the moral-spiritual question of names that enslave. But if as a result dependence is now thought to be unimaginable as anything except servility, the mere reflex of hierarchy, then it is doomed to be stuck with the bad name it has. And so, however subtly, is God the dependent Child, and with that the Trinity altogether.

The bitter connotation that dependence has acquired goes a long way toward explaining our resistance to acknowledging dependence in God. Today more people in the world than not are being pauperized and infantilized as a matter of course, at times to the point of mass starvation and genocide and everywhere to the bereaving of their right to be held accountable for their own history before God. In their case, dependency becomes debasement whether because of their race or age or gender or the disadvantaged position of their nation in the world economy or, if they are fortunate enough to have employment, because of their servile status in a bureaucratic workplace. Further dependencies upon drugs or cheap sex or juvenile pop cultures or armament are only the grosser symptoms of seismic, systemic dependencies made all the more loathsome by a civilization that out of the other side of its mouth pays lip service to initiative and responsibility taking.

It is all too understandable, therefore, that Christian references to God the Son as the supreme dependent would be met with cynicism. Who wouldn't suspect that theological ploy as the ultimate ideological manipulation of a human race already being reduced by itself to massive childishness? But this otherwise warranted suspicion harbors also a monumental self-deception. It provides human beings with an alibi for evading their profoundest, perhaps congenital objection to being dependent. And what is that? Is it pride, *hybris*, *superbia*? Not necessarily.[7] It may be fear, fear of depending. Or it may be that no one is ever good enough at depending, or free enough, to enjoy it. Whatever. In the process what is roundly lost sight of is the magnificent alternative of a whole new dependence which befits not only the liberated creature but "very God." Meanwhile the name that historically occasioned the naming of the Trinity, that is, "Son" or "Child" as a name for God, is resisted even by Christians who might have been counted on to reinstate it. Whether or not the name needs recoining, it surely needs hallowing.

A Bad Question

Nevertheless, the question, at least from the "culture" side of the correlation, persists: Who needs a Child-God who depends, when the supervening need seems rather to be for a God who can be depended upon, whom we can trust to be dependable without being exploitative and arbitrary? Some such culturally based question seems to be presupposed even in the Christian "answers" which from the other side of the correlation have been forthcoming from the theological establishment.[8] In a moment we shall cite as samples the answers from theological liberalism but also from liberalism's presumed antithesis, Barthianism, which at least in their reserve about God the Child are not all that different from each other, and not different enough from the question of their culture to cross-examine it. But first let us note this weakness in the question itself: it underasks.

The question, Who needs a Child-God who depends? underasks not only because it makes God look like a Feuerbachian projection of human need (which "God" so often is) but prior to that, because it seriously underestimates human need. The question suggests that our need of God and of God-talk, including the Trinity, is predominantly a moral need, as if the members of the Trinity are revealed to be interrelated as they are chiefly to enable us to live likewise—trinitarianly, mutually—with one another. That would already be a moralistic reduction not only of the Trinity but of the human plight. But worse, with only that much need of the Trinity, namely, as an inspiration for human communitarianism, the Christian faith loses any compelling reason as to why the "persons" should be related to each other as just parent and child—rather than, say, as lovers or siblings or comrades. Still that was the question to begin with. Is a Child-God necessary?[9]

It is not that the Trinity has no implications for Christian ethos. It does, but not by way of a directly imitable analogy between God and us, and surely not without first providing us with what is otherwise unavailable in this old dependence-averse creation, namely, a whole new substitute order of dependence, transformed and free and effectual, unique with the divine Dependent in Jesus the Christ. Having said that, we must still heed the reminder by a Jürgen Moltmann and the whole Augustinian tradition before him that the triune God is internally a "dynamic community" with lively external consequence for human relations as well.[10] Concede the objection that the New Testament nowhere identifies the Holy Spirit with the *mutuus amor* between Father and Son or that it is reactionary to attribute the divine "begetting" to the Father's need of love. It is still true, as Barbara Brown Zikmund notes, that in trinitarian theology "relationship is fundamental to God and that community is the foundation of God's interaction with the world."[11]

On the other hand, Brown Zikmund's statements that "the doctrine of the Trinity sets forth a radical ethic of justice and care very similar to the ethic that psychologists see within women's lives" and that, thanks to the Trinity, "we are able to live *with*—not just fall down before—our God"[12] may suffer not so much from untruth as from too limited a view of the options. The option that for now seems most wastefully overlooked is the one that addresses a still deeper need, the need for a dependence that not only is not "subjection" to patriarchal "privilege" (far from it) but also is far more basic than mutual, bilateral dependence within community. The sorest need is for that singular dependence of the divine Child upon the Parent, so powerful in its effect that in the process the Parent, indeed the whole Trinity, takes on a new identity and new associations. To ask for less God than that—but now the Christian answer is obviously shaping the question—not only risks moralism but risks underasking.

Theology's "Self-Revealing" Parent

For that matter, the above question, implying the need of God the Parent but not God the Child, might still assume a more than moral need, namely, the need for a prior, viable relation with God. Yet the question still implies by its diminishing of God the Son a merely revelationist diagnosis, one that needs only a parent God who is sufficiently revealing. That weakness appears, for instance, in theological liberalism.[13] Our most pressing need, the revelationist assumes, is for a "self-revelation" from God to which, so the expression goes, we can "relate." As for the relating, which is up to us—faith, absolute dependence, filial hope—that is assumed to be forthcoming so long as the parenting God upholds the initial end of the bargain by being presented, "revealed" winsomely enough—for instance, as maternally tender and caring or for that matter as paternally firm and steady and so on. The rest, our filial response, will then presumably follow, by no means perfectly of course but as well as might be expected.

The point is that what is expected of us in that case as dependents is not all that much, in any case nothing nearly so much as was expected of the biblical-credal Son. For instance, his dependence upon his Father's "begetting" had to survive his very separation from the Father, which he incurred in the first place only because he had obeyed the Father. The old liberal brand of revelationism I am faulting, for all its adherence to Schleiermacher's "absolute dependence," scarcely expects people to be that absolutely dependent, as mortifyingly and surpassingly dependent as the Son is. Nor failing such dependence, are we led to expect the Son to *be* the dependent *for* us, *pro nobis*. But neither is the Son's dependence, whether in our behalf or not, expected to make all that much difference to the identity of God or to God's future.

In theological liberalism, about all that is required of the Son is that by his own filial trust he point us to the God he trusted, the God revealed to be trustworthy of him and by extension of us. And all that is required of us is that by this Jesus-trusted "revelation," by the "disclosive" power of his sonship, we in turn might be "empowered" to emulate his dependence—more and more, perhaps, but more likely, more or less. As often as not, in such accounts, we may have to settle for no more dependence than what Shubert Ogden and David Tracy call "basic beliefs" or for what Santayana called "animal faith."[14] Yet if that minimal dependence suffices to characterize children of God, then there truly does seem to be no life-or-death need for childhood to be godlike, less yet for God to be a child. Thus even the liberal theological establishment, to which we owe so much for its attention to faith (the human analogue of divine dependence) and for its ear to the "culture," is apt to tilt the "correlation" toward this culture's low esteem of dependence and toward a parentalist revelationism.

True, there may be other, more christologically ambitious versions of revelationism than liberalism has traditionally produced. Notably among the Barthians, revelationism has accommodated a Son who at first does seem to do more than reveal a divine fatherliness to our more or less filial responses. With Karl Barth, in fact, the whole Nicene Christology is reactivated. Even so, revelationism is what wins out. In the end, the Son's magnificent dependence is for Barth's God not all that decisive, except as a vehicle for "objectifying" to us the self-revealing divine Subject, the Father, or for "actualizing" among us what for the Father was already the case anyway in his eternal decree of election. God is but "fulfilling His will upon earth as in the eternal decree which precedes everything temporal it is already fulfilled in heaven." Not that the Son is not God; long before he becomes the incarnate object for our knowing he is the eternal Object to the Father. And not that the Son is not dependent; as Object of the Father's self-knowing and self-love he depends on the Father's "positing" him.[15]

However, the effect upon God of the Son's dependence, Barthianism loses: that the Son, precisely as the faithful dependent, all the way to the cross, in turn affects and redefines the very Subject who "begets" him. That God's Dependent, by his very depending, alters the subsequent biography of God, Spirit as well as Father, Barthianism resists. Barth does speak of God's *Menschlichkeit*, humaneness, but only in a way that has always characterized God, all three persons of the Trinity, even before the incarnation. But that God should, as a result of the incarnation, in response to the Child-God's incursion into our kind of dependency, now and forever possess *Menschheit*, human being, within the Trinity itself—that violates Barth's "irreversible sequence."[16]

As for our own dependence as believers, any effort to celebrate the children's faith, paltry as that admittedly is, by such exuberant formulae as *sola fide* encounters in Barthianism a profound reluctance. The fear apparently is that such attention to what the children are doing as children might detract from the sheer gratuitousness of the divine prevenience, and might even reawaken the atheistic anthropocentrism of Ludwig Feuerbach. In Barth's picture of the atonement it is true that the Son altogether intervenes in our behalf, displacing altogether ("overruling") our halfhearted dependence on the Father by his own perfect dependence. Yet the odd conclusion drawn from this intervention is that any subsequent response to all this on our part as believers or as unbelievers, dependents or nondependents, is virtually obviated as unessential to the transaction. At least for now it is, during this pre-Parousia history.[17]

Still, contra Barth, isn't it now exactly when a redeemed dependence on the part of the orphans, their "justifying faith," needs most to be dignified by being told, "O woman, great is your faith" or "Your faith has saved you"? To be sure, that does sound as though dependence, even in its human form called faith, is being deified. And that, for Barth, transgresses "the eschatological limit.[18] So once again, just as in more liberal revelationisms whose Christologies make less cosmic claims, Barthianism too is inclined to undervalue the depending that God's children do, without which the divine Child's depending eludes them.

Orthodoxy's God the Child

Now, it may be that christological and trinitarian dogmas from the early church do not make a point of stressing that the Son is God precisely because of his depending. In fact, they often seem to suggest that he is God in spite of his dependence. There was, after all, the powerful Arian persuasion to contend with, that because the Son is said to be "begotten" (*genneethenta*) he is by definition not God, certainly not "the only true God" of John 17:3, who by contrast is the "unoriginate source" (*agenneetos archee*) of all reality.[19] Up against this well-nigh overwhelming, certainly plausible premise that either God is self-existent or else, if derived, must then be a creature and not God, the orthodox would have had more than enough to do to maintain the simple contrary, that the Son is God *even though* he is begotten.

Nicene Theology

Isn't it achievement enough that the orthodox finally prevailed in showing that the Son is "begotten not made" (*genneethenta ou poieethenta*) and so, as a direct offspring, is "of one substance (*homoousion*) with the Father"? Thus at least they maximized the Son's begottenness in the interest of demonstrating how he is *like* the Father, hence "true God." So what if in the bargain they had to minimize how his begottenness, his dependence, also rendered him *unlike* the Father? They did have to avoid every hint of subordinationism so as not to play into the hands of the Arians. Indeed, the church might well be grateful that they did not regress to the old alternative, much older than Arius's, of affirming the Savior's deity but denying his prenatal sonship.[20] So attractive was the opinion, as now, that God could not be dependent and still be God.

Yet that is not the whole story. It is better than that. Already in their early conflicts with Arianism, but increasingly in subsequent controversy, the orthodox do reflect an interest in locating the Son's deity not only in his likeness with the Father but also in his distinctiveness, that is, in his being an offspring and not the begetter—in our terminology, the dependent and not the one depended upon. For instance, Athanasius cites the Arians's criticism: "If . . . the Son is everlasting and coexists with the Father, then you [Athanasius] are no longer saying that he is the Father's Son but that he is the Father's brother." That might be a plausible objection, Athanasius concedes, if all that the Scriptures said of the Son is that he exists with the Father everlastingly—or even, we might add, if the two were said to be "of the same substance" with *each other*, reciprocally.

However, the *homoousion* is one-directional. The Son is "of one substance with the Father," not the Father of one substance with the Son, reversibly or interchangeably. If the second member, Athanasius retorts, "is the Son—for the Father declares this and the Scriptures shout it out, and 'Son' is nothing other than the begotten from the Father," then the point is made. "The Father is Father and did not become anyone's son;

the Son is Son and not a brother."[21] But see, then, how this Christian insistence on God's being also a dependent Child exposes in the Arians the same religious prejudice we referred to earlier, namely, that such childhood suffers a "bad name," particularly in naming God. Not that the Arians boggled at the name "Son." "They agree with us," Athanasius notes, "about the name of the Son," if only because of its undeniably biblical warrant. What comes down to the same fallacy, however, they say of this Son that "if he is called *God*. He . . . is called so in name only."[22]

But even the name "Son," so Athanasius charged, the Arians begrudged, except as a title of commendation conferred upon the incarnate Word only after his becoming human and taking the "form of a slave," as in Phil. 2:7. For, so argued Arius and Eusebius of Nicomedia and their followers, was it not as "a prize for virtue," a reward of his humble obedience, that the passage says of Christ, "Wherefore God has highly exalted him and given him a name above every name"? But if so, then it was because of this personal "improvement" of his, not prior to his incarnation and humiliation, that "he was called both Son and God" and therefore "is not a true Son." For a "true offspring" is one only "according to nature," by birth, not "by acquisition."[22]

It is instructive to note how, in Athanasius's reply to this exegesis of Philippians 2, he does not accede to the Arian assumption that the title "Son" is a reward for or a recognition of great humility. On the contrary, there is nothing humbling about being the Son, not even the "Son of man." "He being the Son of God became himself the Son of man," but sonship—childhood, dependence—is the "immutable" constant throughout the plot from self-emptying to exaltation and as such *is* not the emptying. A child is not a slave. "So much as the Son differs from a slave, so much the ministry of the Son became better than the ministry of slaves." Slaves are those who are not true children. Slaves not only are not independent but also are not truly dependent. Their "adoption would not happen without the true Son."[24]

If it was not his sonship, his being a dependent child—and perhaps not even his becoming human qua human—which constituted the Son's humiliation, then what did? Answer: his becoming our *kind* of human, enslaved and terminal. That, according to Athanasius, is what Philippians 2 intends by "the form of the slave." The Son, for whom it was already sheer glory to be a Son, "humbled himself in taking our humble body [humble because it was "flesh," and "death was in need of this" flesh] and took the form of a slave when he put on the flesh enslaved to sin."[25]

Contrary to the Arians, therefore, the Son is subsequently exalted not in his sonship, which needed no such "improvement," but the exaltation is of the humanity. It is said "about the human nature." "Therefore humanly, because of the flesh which he bore, it is said about him, 'Lift up the gates' and 'he will come in,' as if a man enters."[26] One is reminded of the statement by Luther:

> According to our calendar Jesus the son of Mary is 1543 years old this year. But from the moment that the deity and the humanity were united in one person this man, Mary's son, is and is called the almighty and everlasting God.[27]

Similarly, Dorothy L. Sayers said it is only the Christians' God who has a date in history.[28] If so, the Trinity, though forever triune, has not been the same since, all as a result of God the Child's very consequential dependence.

For Athanasius, what is good news about this is that the slavish (not filial) flesh which the Son put on is our own, just as it is our own therefore which in him is "sanctified" and "exalted" and "deified." "He deified that which he put on, and more, he offered this to the human race." "In his death we all have died in Christ so that in Christ himself again we may be highly exalted, being raised from the dead and rising into heaven."[29]

The felicitous continuity between Christ and ourselves consists not only in his being human as we but also prior to his humanity, his being a Child as we too are meant to be. It is of the nature of the Son, being derived, to "receive." (Even as a God who "gives" he gives only "from the Father." But notice, "his Father is [not] the one who became flesh.") That is also our nature, to receive. This is clear from our very bodiliness, for "a body . . . by nature is a receiver of grace."[30] In the Son, therefore, we are exalted to true receivers, true bodies, true dependents. Much later, but in the same spirit, the Formula of Concord would exhort Christians to "rejoice constantly that our flesh and blood have in Christ been made to sit so high at the right hand of the majesty and almighty power of God."[31]

Post-Nicene Theology

The Cappadocians, too, reflect interest not only in the Son's deity but also in the deity's sonship, his childlike dependence *as God*. For that is prerequisite to his subsequent childlike dependence as human being, if he is to "deify" the dependence or childhood of fallen human beings. He, "the one which depends," is even described as "caused." He is the one who is "from the cause" by contrast with God the Parent, who is the "cause." But again, the fact that "the ground of unity [is] the Father, out of whom and towards whom the subsequent persons are reckoned," in no way renders these "subsequent persons," the Son and the Holy Spirit, anything else but God. Being "caused" is as much a divine hypostasis as is the parenting "cause."[32]

Moreover, these three hypostases are a unity in the way they "cooperate"—close ranks, so to speak, and present a common front—in a "single operation" or "action" (*energeia*) "in every activity which pervades from God to creation." Consider, says Gregory of Nyssa, the divine gift we call life. "Though we presuppose that there are three persons and names, we do not reason that three lives have been given to us—individually one from each of them. It is the same life activated by the Holy Spirit, prepared by the Son, and produced by the Father's will."[33] Notice, for our present theme, "prepared by the Son." His very sonship, his filial dependence is indispensable to the single action of the Trinity as a whole. In everything that God does to and with and in creation, the divine childhood is prerequisite and is powerfully determinative.

What is more, though Gregory of Nyssa said that it is by the Father that the Son is "caused," the senior Gregory of Nazianzus could go further and locate a "cause" also outside God, namely, in our "salvation." Evidently it is so characteristic of the Son to be "caused"—or, as we have been saying, to be dependent—that it comes as no violation of his deity to be conditioned also by this "later," human, inner-historical cause. What is "this cause"? Says Gregory to his critics, It is "the salvation of insolent you, you who on this account despised his deity so that he received your materiality." He "became a human being," "so that I might become God as he became man."[34]

But on closer examination of Gregory's language we note that the One who is "caused" by our salvation seems to be not just the Son but the one "God," Godself. Since our salvation is the unitary action of the one Godhead, therefore what had been the unique circumstance of the Son, namely, being caused, now extends to the Trinity as a whole. Isn't that what Gregory is here implying? "In the beginning he was without cause, for who is the cause of God? But later because of a cause (namely, our salvation) he came into existence." Who did? The One who "became a human being," of course, the Son. Yet in his doing so, who else is it but God, whole and entire, who thereby becomes as Gregory says, "the God below"?[35] That influential, that God-definining is God the Child in his filial achievement.

Are we pressing the words of Gregory of Nazianzus beyond their intention? He does seem to include the above argument among what he calls "riddles," calculated to silence the "logic-choppers."[36] On the other hand, elsewhere he makes a related point in a way that leaves small doubt about his intention. As the Word became flesh "for the sake of my flesh, and conjoins himself with an intelligent soul for my soul's sake, . . . and in all points, sin excepted, becomes man," what is it that the Word is thereby doing? Answer: he "comes to his own image," "cleansing like by like."[37] It cannot be much of a stretch to infer that we are the Word's "image" not only by virtue of having "flesh" and "intelligent soul" but also by being, as the Word is, dependent children, though we as "made" and he as "begotten." As God the Child comes to the world's orphans, the would-be children, he "comes to his own image." And as the Word assumes our fallen dependency, he is "cleansing like by like," the "like" in this case being God's own childhood analogous to ours. Such an evangelical claim Gregory would hardly begrudge in view of his famous formula, "What has not been assumed cannot be restored; it is what is united with God that is saved."[38]

Another way in which post-Nicene orthodoxy, after the Cappadocians, asserts the point is in its denying that there are "two sons." Whether or not Nestorius, for instance, actually taught that error, Cyril of Alexandria definitely perceived him to be so inclined. When, as Cyril saw Nestorius doing, we so distinguish within Christ as "to say that on the one hand there is a proper human being who is dignified with the *title* of 'Son,' while on the other hand, there is the proper Logos of God, who possesses by *nature* both the name and the exercise of sonship," then "we fall into the assertion of two Sons." It is not enough, Cyril continues, "to allege that there is a union of persons, for Scripture says not that the Logos united to himself the person of a human being but that he became flesh." The Son of God "became (*egeneto*) a human being and has been designated 'Son of Man' "—"one Son out of two." The unity of his pre-incarnate childhood with our kind of childhood must be indissoluble, "for us and for our salvation."[39]

Even in his second letter to Cyril, Nestorius still seems to me to be justifying the former's suspicions. "It is obvious," Nestorius insists, "that the son of David was not the divine Logos." Reference is made to Matt. 22:42-44, in which Jesus asks, "What do you think about the Christ? Whose son is he?" Since as Jesus' critics agree, the Christ is the son of David, Jesus then continues, how could the psalmist David refer to an offspring of his the way he does, as "Lord"? Exactly. The two are one and the same. To be an offspring, even an offspring of the human David, does not prevent him from being—on the contrary, in this case qualifies him to be—"Lord." The Child, precisely by being the Child he is, human as well as divine, is Lord. And isn't that "the Lord your God" who, only a moment before, Jesus' critics had unwittingly agreed should be loved "with all your heart and soul and mind"? Still, Nestorius's short-falling answer still beggars the question, "He is entirely the son of David according to the flesh but Lord according to the deity."[40]

Nestorius finds it abhorrent "to make the divine Logos have a part in being fed with milk and participate to some degree in growth and stand in need of angelic assistance because of his fearfulness at the time of the passion, [to] say nothing about circumcision and sacrifice and tears and hunger." "These things are taken falsely when they are put off on the deity." Admittedly Nestorius's concern, that "the things peculiar to the natures within the unitary sonship [must] not get endangered by the suggestion of a confusion," was a warranted concern,[41] and his warnings were not lost even in the Chalcedonian "Definition of the Faith" which condemned him. Nevertheless his error did need to be countered, as it was in the Formula of Reunion (433 C.E.): God the Son who "was born from the Father . . . [is] *the same one* [who] was born . . . from Mary the Virgin. . . . This *same one* is coessential with the Father, as to his deity, and coessential with us, as to his humanity . . . , 'one Son'!" "The very same One."[42] So "does God have a mother," and a quite human one? Chalcedon left no doubt: God the child does, as all children do.

The Trinity's Namesakes

If there are those who because of Christ now enjoy an altogether new and liberated dependence, how should they be named? Offhand it would seem natural to call them his codependents. Unfortunately, as in Anne Wilson Schaef's sobering book by that name, codependence is now a clinical term describing "a disease within the addictive process"[43]—one more instance of the bad name that dependence has so

widely and deservedly acquired. Alternatively the new God-relation in
Christ might be called the New Childhood were that not so close to "second childhood," which again connotes senility and childishness, only
encouraging the illusion that being children, daughters and sons, must
mean not being adults. It is childlikeness of course, not childishness,
which God the Child embodies and confers. It is that fully responsible
maturity which Dietrich Bonhoeffer called *Mündigkeit*, "coming of age."
For him that was unthinkable without "faith," than which nothing in all
of life could be more dependent. But then, must those with faith, the
Trinity's newly mature dependents, remain nameless?

For now they may have to be content with the baptismal tradition,
going under that name into which they have been christened, the triune
name. Yet the marvelous audacity which is implied in so naming them is
easily overlooked and degenerates into formality. The need is urgent to
republicize the godlike dignity of their dependence which the baptismal
title implies. But doing that, naming them in a manner that in our culture
communicates the honor to which their divine childhood is entitled is as
difficult as naming their triune God, and for much the same reason.
What Sandra Schneiders prescribes for "the long process of conversion
from the idolatry of maleness" applies also, perhaps more so, to the long
process of renaming trinitarian dependence. She calls it a project in
"conversion," in "spirituality"—that is, in "our *experience* of God"—in
"healing." And it is "the imagination [which] must be healed." For "it is
the imagination which creates our God-image and our self-image."[44]

But what if, sounding hauntingly like Feuerbach, it is from our self-
image that our God-image must be derived? For Christians that is con-
ceivable if, as Gregory of Nazianzus said of the incarnation, God "comes
to his image," "cleansing like with like." If our childish dependence, demeaned and accursed though it is, harbors our *imago Dei* and if God the
Child is "like" for our "like," then in that respect our self-image as children is where the God-image of the Child meets itself coming back. On
the other hand, if our image of ourselves as dependent children is by
now so debased as to be an object of scorn, what further need is there of
evidence of divine wrath? Schneiders is right: what is demanded is conversion, a spiritual healing of our images, but images not in the sense
merely of our mental pictures but of our personal resemblance to God.
We do name God on the basis of a real *analogia entis*, of something in
ourselves. Yet if that is missing, we draw a blank. Then God remains

nameless, but so do we. We need to *become* children like God if we are to *re-cognize* the God who is a Child.

The Holying Spirit, the Re-Imager

Spiritual healing of our images is a task that dare not exclude that member of the Trinity of whom we have so far said little, the Spirit, who is distinguished as "Holy," that is, as holying, hallowing, healing.[45] In the history of trinitarian theology there are two classic issues about the Holying Spirit that pertain particularly to our theme. The first, by no means obvious, stresses that she is a person, not just a neuter, impersonal principle of power, however divine and life-giving and fruits-bearing— merely a source of empowerment.[46] By "person" all we need to mean at this point is that she is Godself or, as we might say, God "in person." Recall Paul's analogy: "After all, the depths of a person (*anthrōpou*) can only be known by that person's own spirit, not by any other person, and in the same way the depths of God can only be known by the Spirit of God" (1 Cor. 2:11). Nothing less than God's self can so hallow ourselves that they can once again "image" God. "God's Spirit joins itself to our spirits to declare that we are God's children" (Rom. 8:16).

Those who have been Spirited into echoing the divine claim upon them that they are "God's children" have what Paul calls "the mind of Christ" (1 Cor. 2:16). That brings us to the second trinitarian issue involving the Holying Spirit: contrary to first impressions, for all her inseparable identification with Christ, she *is* not Christ, even the glorified Christ now present in the church. If the pun did not smack of tritheism we might say she is a "person" in her own right. Yet her distinctiveness from God the Child is meant to protect his distinctiveness as well. Else the temptation, as in revelationism, is to imagine that it is especially his role to reveal God the Parent when in fact he needs quite as much to be revealed as the Parent does.[47] Where would he have gotten in the world, hence where would we, without Pentecost? It was a brand of revelationism which the Augsburg Confession attacks, "that the Word and the Holy Spirit are not necessarily distinct persons but that the Word signifies a physical [incarnate] word or voice and that the Holy Spirit is a [responsive] movement induced in creatures."[48]

Conversely, neither is she the dependent God the Child who became one of us. Nor is that her claim. It is one of the finer amusements in the history of theology that neither Gregory of Nazianzus nor Augustine, once they had discovered that the Holy Spirit is as consubstantially derived from the Godhead as the Son is, could then explain how her "procession" differs from the "generation" of the Son.[49] It simply is not the point of her name, as it is with the "only-begotten Son's," to characterize her in terms of her dependence, though undoubtedly that is a deducible conclusion. Excessive speculation about her inner-*trinitarian* relations risks invading her privacy but also distorting her inner-*worldly* image.

It should be enough to know that though the Father sends her in response to the Son's request and promise and though it is the Son's words and deeds which she promotes and illumines, touting his strange lordship, though only and always as cruciform son, her special mission is to proceed. She proceeds usward, toward the slavish orphans, with the gift of their own new childhood, starting with their faith. In that faith lies their image, self-image as well as God-image. The children's "life" from the one God, recalling Gregory of Nyssa, while it is "produced by the Father's will" and "prepared by the Son" is finally and climactically "activated by the Holy Spirit." *Dea volente*. Else not at all.

"Abba," In Whose Image

In rebirthing them, the Holy Spirit introduces the children to their new Parent, emboldening them to call out, "Abba, Father" (Rom. 8:15; Gal. 4:6). It requires little imagination to guess where she (or Paul) got that term of endearment for the divine Parent. Clearly it comes from Jesus' own innovative, startling usage. By now it should no longer be necessary (though alas it is) to demonstrate that Jesus' addressing God as "Abba" and "Father" hardly implies that God is male, any more than the pre-incarnate "Son" is or than the Holying Spirit is female or neuter, much less implies that God is patriarchal.[50] Nor, I think, does Joachim Jeremias's research on this subject compel the conclusion that "Abba-Father" is the normative Christian address to God.[51] Not if "normative" means compulsory, reducing Jesus' usage to legal precedent. Still, the fact that "Abba-Father" does characterize Jesus' distinctive relationship to God opens a larger question (as feminist theologies to their credit have repeatedly done): What does it mean to say that Jesus the Christ's relationship to God is—not only reveals or empowers but *is*—our own relationship to God?

A case in point is the difficulty that Christians have, also Christian feminists, in calling God the Parent "Mother," that is, if it is to be the same God who parents Jesus Christ. For Jesus very much had a mother,

Mary. But she, being only human, was not his God or anyone else's. The one father he acknowledged, the only one he promised to others, is God the Father. From the apostles onward "Father" has been interchangeable, indeed synonymous, with "the Father of our Lord Jesus Christ." Accordingly, Christians can speak of God as "Mother" only with considerable abstractness, disengaged from the incarnation, at least never interchangeably with "the mother of our Lord Jesus Christ." This difficulty has nothing necessarily to do with overcoming sexist speech haibts or with vestigial patriarchalism or with reverence for Jesus' religious experience and linguistic mannerisms. The difficulty, presuming it inheres in Jesus' very parentage, might possibly be relieved by altering the traditional accounts of who he was, for instance, by insisting he (as we) did have a natural father. But there is little enthusiasm for that, at least publicly. And if there were, wouldn't that only confirm how deeply Christians prize being parented by the same God, however named, by which Christ is parented? That pathos is hard to conceal and should not be trivialized, least of all by patriarchalists.

Diane Tennis has set Christians a provocative question with her book *Is God the Only Reliable Father?*[52] On one count, at least, the answer to her question must be yes. But then that is not only humbling for all other, unreliable fathers or parents generally. It is at least as humbling for them as sons and daughters, as those who are to do the relying. For in the suspenseful story of the Trinity, the one Father on whom God the Child is expected to rely, and wondrously does rely, would defy the confidence of even the most trusting human child. Even poor Isaac, not to mention his parents, was at the last moment spared the mortifying test of filial dependence endured by his prototype, who "for our sake was crucified under Pontius Pilate, suffered death and was buried" yet through it all "trusted the One who judges justly" (1 Peter 2:23). The outcome, that the Child "on the third day rose again in accordance with the Scriptures, ascended into heaven and is seated on the right hand of the Father," does vindicate the latter as the only reliable Parent—at least of Christ. But is the Father the only reliable Parent of Christ's siblings? That can be only if *Christ's* filial dependence is what gives *theirs* its value. Only then does his Childhood come full thrust, in their faith in his depending for them, making him "the firstborn of all creation." Only then does the One whose "image" he is become the mothering "Abba" of everyone else (Col. 1:12ff.).

The Next "Mythic Image"?

Maybe patriarchy is diminishing, after all, slowly to be replaced by its ironic opposite, what Stanley Kunitz discerns as a growing trend in twentieth-century American poetry, "the mythic image of the absent father":

> He has died of natural causes, or by suicide, or in the wars of the century. . . . With the disintegration of the nuclear family, the symbol of the father as a dominant, or domineering, presence is fading away. Whole sections of our nation are living in fatherless homes as a result of death, illegitimacy, divorce or abandonment. Even when he is physically present in the household, the father may be spiritually absent, separated from his children by the acceleration of the historical process in our time, particularly true in an advanced technological society and one with large immigrant enclaves.

Or "often," says Kunitz, "the father is more than absent; he is lost, as he has been lost to himself for most of his adult life, crushed by his burdens, rendered impotent by fatigue and anxieties, reduced to a number, a statistical integer, in the army or the factory or the marketplace."[53]

What if, post patriarchy, the next project in image-healing, in hallowing the name, will be "the absent father"—the absent Father. Then wouldn't a trinitarianism that celebrates the sheer glorious deity of the Child, as we have been urging, only further upstage and distance the Father from the world? That is a risk, especially if the second person of the Trinity continues to be re-imaged as a sort of surrogate Parent, distorting the very childlike, *ebed Yahweh* genius of his "lordship." On the other hand, it is exactly this "way to the Father, "through the child who among us experienced something of fatherlessness at firsthand, that also God the Parent recovers the good family name through the healing Spirit. Maybe Oscar Cullmann overstated the case: "Because the first-century Christian believes in Christ as Lord, he believes in God and in the Holy Spirit." But Pierre Benoit's retort to Cullmann, though true, is hardly less extravagant: "It is because the Christian believes in the Father who raised him and in the Spirit whose outpouring manifests his triumph, that he believes in Jesus the Lord." In any case, as Benoit says, "It is true that the Father and the Spirit are generally considered in the context of the Son's work."[54] A remarkable "Subordinate." Remarkable connections.

MISSIOLOGICAL NAMING: "WHO SHALL I SAY SENT ME?"

> Since we are forbidden here to use the holy name in support of false-
> hood or wickedness, it follows, conversely, that we are commanded to
> use it in the service of truth and all that is good.
>
> Martin Luther, Large Catechism

*I*n 1963 the then General Secretary of the World Council of Churches,
the late W. A. Visser 't Hooft, wrote a slim volume entitled *No Other
Name: The Choice Between Syncretism and Christian Universalism.*[1] One
of its title pages contained the text from Acts 4:12: "And there is salvation
in no one else, for there is no other name under heaven given among
men by which we must be saved." *No Other Name* contained a ringing attack on theological syncretism and a staunch defense of christocentric
universalism as the sole basis for the church's continued missionary
effectiveness.

Recently a Catholic theologian, Paul Knitter, published a book with
a title similar to the one by Visser 't Hooft but significantly ending with
a question mark: *No Other Name? A Critical Survey of Christian Attitudes
Toward the World Religions.*[2] The diacritical difference implied by Knitter's
question mark was no accident, for his own position rejects the "one and
only" exclusivist Christology championed by Visser 't Hooft in favor of a
softer, more inclusive approach. For Knitter, "no other name" is the language of personal commitment rather than ultimate truth. His argument
ends by admitting the possibility of other incarnations and salvation options, thus effectively undercutting the urgency of proclaiming the gospel of salvation through faith in Jesus Christ.

The two contrasting book titles serve in some way to highlight the subject of this essay: that salvation history witnesses to a procession of divinely appointed agents sent to do God's bidding, culminating in the coming of the unique "Son" of God, "Jesus," "Emmanuel," the "Lord of Lords" and "King of Kings," in whose holy name salvation is to be proclaimed to the ends of the earth. Our subject is sending and going out in the powerful name of One who embodies God's unique promise and gift of salvation.

Sending and Naming

The title of this chapter has been derived from the account in Exodus 3 of the appearance of the angel of the Lord in a burning bush to Moses at Horeb and of God's commission to Moses to "bring forth my people . . . out of Egypt." The Lord is revealed to Moses beside the burning bush as "the God of your father, the God of Abraham, the God of Isaac, and the God of Jacob" (Exod. 3:6). The text continues:

> And now, behold, the cry of the people of Israel has come to me, and I have seen the oppression with which the Egyptians oppress them. Come, I will send you to Pharaoh that you may bring forth my people, the sons of Israel, out of Egypt. (Exod. 3:9-10)

The timid Moses demurs, raising in succession *four* objections to carrying out Yahweh's commission. "Who am I that should go to Pharaoh, and bring the sons of Israel out of Egypt?" asks Moses. "But I will be with you," God replies, offering as a "sign" that when the people of Israel have been delivered from Egypt they will make a pilgrimage to Horeb to serve God upon the very mountain beside which Moses received his commission.

There follows Moses' second objection to undertaking God's commission: he does not even know the *name* of the God who is sending him, and thus his mission will be undermined by lack of credibility.

Then Moses said to God, "If I come to the people of Israel and say to them, 'The God of your fathers has sent me to you,' and they ask me, 'What is his name?' what shall I say to them?" God said to Moses, "I AM WHO I AM." And he said, "Say this to the people of Israel, 'I AM has sent me to you.' " God also said to Moses, "Say this to the people of Israel, 'The Lord, the God of your fathers, the God of Abraham, the God of Isaac, and the God of Jacob, has sent me to you': this is my name for ever, and thus I am to be remembered throughout all generations" (Exod. 3: 13-15).

We observe here, apparently for the first time in Scripture, a close link between the God who *sends* Moses on a divine commission to free God's people and the revelation of the *name* of God under whose authority Moses is sent. The linkage between divine *sending* and the revelation of the divine *name* provides the inspiration for the subtitle of this essay, "Missiological Naming." It will be our task to determine as far as possible the precise implications of conjoining these two concepts.

We need not at this stage be concerned with Moses' other objections (Exod. 4:1, 10) to God's commission or with the striking contrasts between the JE version of Moses' call cited above (Exodus 3) and the later Priestly version (Exodus 6). Our aim will be to determine whether missiological naming occurs with sufficient frequency and prominence in biblical literature to warrant closer attention from a theological and linguistic point of view or whether it can be dismissed as an isolated instance.

Do revelation and invocation of the divine name inevitably suggest the notion of authoritative sending in the witness of Scripture as a whole? Does divine sending or commissioning to special service as prophet, apostle, or other divine emissary rely, according to biblical evidence, on the supernatural power inherent in the name of God for its efficacy and fulfillment? If such a relationship does indeed exist, what was the experience of the early church with regard to missiological naming? And how is the relation between the divine name and authoritative sending reflected in Christian tradition and in the life of the Christian community today? We shall want to consider whether "naming the name" of God (or of the Trinity or Jesus Christ) continues to evoke a response of "sending" or "outreach" today.

Does an indispensable link exist between the public use of God-language and the call to service, that is, the response of mission, such that as soon as one evokes the name of deity one can no longer avoid the impulse to "go" for the purpose of witness or service? Or can the public use of God-language be considered a neutral activity that carries no necessary obligation to "do" the will of God whose name is invoked? Do worship and liturgy, for example, with their repeated use of God-language in creed and liturgical text, constitute an irrefusable call to mission? What about preaching, teaching, or lecturing with reference to God-language: does each mention of the sacred name of deity constitute a fresh commissioning to some aspect of divine service? May it not, at the very least, prompt fresh reflection on the meaning of Christian calling and sending for both speaker and listener?

The pastoral, professional, vocational, and existential implications of missiological naming must be explored if this inquiry is to go beyond the mere collecting of biblical data. The question is not merely one of whether Moses or Isaiah responded to the divine call and allowed themselves to be sent in the divine name in times past, or whether the early apostles in Jerusalem "named the name" of the risen Christ in justifying their subversive activities before the court of the Sanhedrin in Jerusalem.

The deeper, probing question for Christians today is whether we have been seduced into the secular habit of robbing God-language of its missiological significance. Do we who "know" the name of God evacuate it of its powerful significance as a "call" to "go" and manifest the divine power and glory? Do we treat the divine name as mere sound or syllable having no power of its own to judge, command, forgive, or heal? In short, does the public use of God-language in our modern culture continue to function as a hypostasis of divine being, power, and living presence—in Paul Tillich's language, as a symbol that participates in the "ground of being"—or has it become a mere acoustical noise that denominates some "object" present in our environment or mental consciousness? Related to this is the question of whether contemporary Christians have not often bought into the secular habit of treating references to God with skepticism and incredulity, to be received in a spirit of levity and with impunity. For when Christians capitulate to secular conventions in making profane use of the name of God, they reject biblical warnings against misusing the divine name. This constitutes a separate indictment that goes beyond the scope of the present essay.

Problems in Approaching the Subject

At the outset it is well to recognize serious impediments to a responsible approach to the study of missiological naming. The writer has not been able to find any pioneer studies that point the way. The subject as presented seems to be a virtual novelty. The approach to the subject through word studies of biblical key words as found in theological dictionaries of the Old and New Testaments yields useful data which are nevertheless, in the final analysis, rather inconclusive. No specific biblical word studies bring together the key terms of "naming" and "sending," as I am attempting to do in this essay. Moreover, the task would seem to require a competent biblical exegete familiar with both Hebrew and Greek texts and with the intertestamental literature. The task, if competently carried out, should also have an interdisciplinary character in view of the church historical and systematic theological aspects of the question. The writer, moreover, makes no claims to expertise in regard to contemporary researches into God-language.

It may be supposed that the discipline of missiology could throw some particularly useful light on the subject of missiological naming. Even here, however, difficulties exist. A missiological effort to disclose the biblical and theological meaning of missiological naming must be undertaken in close dependence on the findings of biblical exegetes. Here, however, we must take note of an unfortunate gap—an absence of close interaction—between biblical scholarship on the one hand and the contemporary study of missiology. The International Association of Mission Studies (IAMS) has for some time carried on a project designated as Biblical Studies and Missiology (BISAM) for the precise purpose of promoting closer dialogue and interdependence between the two disciplines.[3] The project thus far demonstrates that very considerable difficulties are involved in moving from an analysis of biblical data to usable missiological conclusions.

David Bosch, a noted missiologist from South Africa, draws attention to the different perspectives and methodologies of biblical scholars and missiologists that stand in the way of their collaboration:

> Biblical scholars, on the whole, tend to emphasize the diversity of the biblical message and the historical conditioning of each text. This makes them very reticent to draw a direct connection between the biblical text and today's missionary enterprise. The biblical text functions, at most, as a metaphor, model or paradigm for our own involvement, and there always remains a large range of alternative possibilities; we should, therefore, refrain from any single-option reductionism. In addition, biblical scholars tend to point out that the books of the Bible were not written as guides for Christian mission (not even the *Book of Acts*) so they cannot become that twenty centuries later. The reticence of biblical scholars thus indeed helps us to come to a fuller understanding of the text in its original historical setting. At the same time, however, they frequently fail to show whether, and, if so, how, the Bible can be of significance to the church-in-mission and how, if at all, a connection between the biblical evidence and the contemporary missionary scene can be made. The church thus feels left in the lurch, at least to a degree.

By contrast *missiologists* writing on the "biblical foundations for mission" tend to err in the opposite direction. Even where they are sufficiently sophisticated not to use the Bible as a handy reference file of quotations to justify their own group's actions, they do have a tendency to operate with a very large brush. On the one hand, they are inclined to overlook the rich diversity of the biblical record and therefore to reduce the biblical motivation for mission to one single idea or text (for instance, the great commission or, more recently in Liberation theology circles, Jesus' appeal to Isaiah in Luke 4); on the other hand, they tend far too easily to read back into the Bible aspects of the missionary enterprise in which they are involved today.[4]

A further word of caution is voiced by Walter Brueggemann, a noted Old Testament scholar. His guiding assumption is clear:

Scripture study, always in protest against the tendency of theological reductionism to which the church is tempted, must stress diversity. Church practice, whether in systematic theology, missions or homiletics, tends to reduce the Bible to a set of simple moves which can be made in an identifiable, predictable way. Against that, Scripture study must insist on a range of alternative moves which remain in deep tension with each other but are all biblical. The Scripture scholar is most helpful to colleagues when this range of alternatives is explored and assessed in critical ways.[5]

Brueggemann adds:

Students of mission would do well to discern the rich alternative possibilities in Scripture that rescue us from any single-option reductionism.[6]

A Catholic theologian, Robert Schreiter, supports Brueggemann's view that there are no simple or obvious moves from the Bible to contemporary mission motivation, strategy, or practice. He speaks of the Bible's role in provoking meaning, opening horizons, envisioning possibilities, or as an invitation to experience the full range of meanings present to present-day readers:

Whether we see the role of the Bible for mission as engaging us in command, strategy or the imagination, we are invited in each instance to ask again the question, What is our relation to the text? . . . This reminds us of how much our interests and our social context shape our searching of the Scriptures, our discernment of biblically based mission plans or models of church growth. . . . The sensitivity to context, both the Bible's and our own, has made us realize to what extent the social setting shapes our reading of the Bible. We talk increasingly in terms of *models* of faith and culture—that is, different ways of interaction between Christian belief and practice, and specific cultural settings.[7]

A common theme of these commentators has been the complexity of the hermeneutical task as it applies to the practice of mission, and the need to understand and respect the methodological scruples of Scripture scholars, and by extension those of systematic theologians and church historians as well. Sensitive to this line of reasoning, many missiologists have given up the effort to base missiological thinking on a single foundational theme such as "sending" or "witness," knowing that any theme selected for that purpose will be qualified by other viewpoints and perspectives. Missiologists within the ecumenical movement, insofar as they deal with biblical foundations, are now more likely to be engaged in exploring a range of alternative options that address, partially at least, the basis and goal of Christian mission. There exists today no normative biblical understanding of "sending." This makes any effort to develop an adequate biblical and theological exposition of missiological naming a tentative and rather precarious undertaking. Even so, some examination of the biblical data on divine *naming* and *sending* will be necessary to establish the appropriateness of juxtaposing the two key terms in the title phrase "missiological naming."

Biblical Data on the Divine Name and Naming

A biblical word study of Hebrew and Greek usage of "name" and "naming" underscores the frequency with which "name" or the "name of God" occurs in the literature of the Old and New Testaments. The 770 singular and 84 plural occurrences of "name" in the Old Testament suggest that it is a biblical concept or key word of some prominence.[8]

Names in the Bible, whether of God or of human beings, have more than denotative significance; they are also rich in theological meaning, divine empowerment, and prediction. The most common biblical understanding of "sending," to be examined more fully below, is that one is commissioned to speak or act in the name and power of God.

In biblical literature, to give a name is to establish power or control over someone or something. To call upon a name is to place someone under the protection of the person invoked. Proper names—for example, "Moses" or "Jesus"—establish the identities of their bearers. To give someone a "new name" is to bestow a new status (Gen. 32:28; Isa. 62:2, 4). God reveals one of many divine names to Abraham (El Shaddai, Gen. 17:1), another to Moses (YHWH, Exod. 3:15; cf. 6:2). God hears when properly called upon, but God's name is a gift of revelation, not an instrument of magic or for incantation. Invocation of God's name implies faith in God's power, for example, in swearing, cursing, or blessing. God's name may be given to a place, for example, the temple, as a pledge of God's saving presence. After the exile, the divine name often denotes the "glory of God." In later literature the name of God is often hypostatized, that is, made to stand alongside God as an acting subject or instrument of divine will. God raises up prophets to speak God's words "in my name" (Deut. 18:15, 19), that is, on the commission of God.

In the New Testament, the name, person, and work of God are inseparably linked to those of Jesus Christ (Mark 11:9-10; Matt. 23:39). The revelation of the name of God is linked to the glorification of God (John 12:28). God's name is glorified in the life, work, death, and resurrection of Jesus Christ (John 17:1-2, 6-7); the Father glorifies the Son, and the Son glorifies the Father through the manifestation of the divine name. Jesus discloses the intimate name of God (Father, Holy Father: John 17:1, 5, 11, 21, 24, 25; cf. Matt. 6:8-9; Luke 11:2), giving it new content. To be received "in Jesus' name" is to stand in the sphere of the love of Father and Son (John 17:11-12, 21). Glorifying God's name is Christ's work in terms of both revelation and reconciliation.

The fullness of Christ's work and identity is demonstrated in the various names of the Nazarene: "Jesus" (lit., "Savior," "he will save," Matt. 1:21), "Emmanuel" ("God with us," Matt. 1:23), "Son" of God (Heb. 1:4), "Lord" ("the name above every name," Phil. 2:9-11), "King of kings" and "Lord of lords" (Rev. 19:16). Jesus' names embrace the whole content of God's saving acts: baptism, sanctification, and justification (see 1 Cor. 6:11). Thus Peter can say that "there is salvation in no one else, for there is *no other name* under heaven given among human beings by which we must be saved" (Acts 4:12). The Father sends the Spirit in the name of Jesus (John 14:16).

In the Matthean Great Commission, Father, Son and Spirit come together and give fullness to the Father's name (Matt. 28:19). Baptism into the triune name means entering into fellowship with the Father through the Son and coming under the operation of the Spirit. Gathering in Christ's name (Matt. 18:20) is meeting in the presence of Christ. The Lord's Prayer (Matt. 6:9; Luke 11:2) is a prayer that God will sanctify the divine name in spite of opposition. The disciples are urged to pray in Jesus' name (John 14:13-14), that is, according to Jesus' specific mandate and promise. The unity of Father and Son is shown in the Son's power to effect whatever the disciples ask in his name.

Believing in Jesus' name (John 2:23) means believing in him as Christ, the Word who was with God from the beginning (John 1:12); those who believe in this name receive power to become children of God. Believers in the name of Christ can act according to Christ's commission and with divine power (Luke 10:17); even nondisciples can on occasion cast out demons in Jesus' name (Luke 9:49). Little ones are received in Jesus' name (Matt. 18:5). The lame are healed in the name of Jesus of Nazareth (Acts 3:6, 16).

The name of Jesus is the basis and theme of missionary proclamation (Acts 8:12). Repentance is to be preached to the Gentiles in the name of Jesus (Luke 24:47). Saul at first opposes the name of Jesus of Nazareth (Acts 26:9) but after his conversion proclaims it (Acts 9:27-29), and speaks of his commission to "bring about the obedience of faith for the sake of his name among all the nations" (Rom. 1:5). Belief in the name leads to confession of it (Phil. 2:11), suffering for it ("for my sake," Mark 10:29; "on my account," John 15:21). Disciples rejoice to suffer dishonor for Jesus' name (Acts 5:41), and Paul and Barnabas risk their lives for the sake of Jesus (Acts 15:26). The saints in heaven are rewarded for fearing Christ's name (Rev. 11:18). Singing the song of Moses and of the Lamb, they glorify the name of the Lord, "for thou alone art holy" (Rev. 15:4). In Antioch for the first time the name of Christ is given to "Christians" (Acts 11:26).

In sum, the divine name functions as a comprehensive symbol for the power, presence, and saving purpose of God. The mission of Jesus is to manifest the divine name to the world. Already from his infancy, the name of Jesus is associated with God's saving purpose for the world. During his earthly lifetime, Jesus instructs the disciples to call on God as "Father," and even to call on the Father in his (Jesus') name. After his resurrection and glorification, the apostles are sent out to make disciples of all nations and to proclaim salvation in the name of the triune God.

Biblical Data on Divine Sending

In the Old Testament, the concept of divine sending is prominent in the Pentateuchal literature and the prophets. God calls and sends Abraham (Gen. 12:1), Moses (Exod. 3:10), the prophet Nathan (2 Sam. 12:1),

Elijah (1 Kings 17:8; 18:1; 19:11, 15; 21:18), Isaiah (Isa. 6:8, 9), Jeremiah (Jer. 2:1), Ezekiel (Ezek. 2:3, 3:4), and Jonah (Jonah 1:2). The mission of the "Servant of the Lord" (Isa. 42: 1-4; 49:1-6; 50:4-11; 52:13—53:12) embodies the notion of sending, first to Israel and then to the nations, to bring God's teaching and restore justice. The Servant's mission is closely identified with manifesting the name of the Lord and giving light to the nations (Isa. 42:6-8), and it foreshadows the sending of Jesus as the bearer of a new covenant.

In the New Testament, *apostellō* functions as a strengthened compound of *stellō* (= "to send") and carries the idea of divine commission and authorization, that is, of an official envoy or divinely sent teacher who embodies the will of the sender. *Apostellō* occurs 135 times in the New Testament, mostly in the Gospels and Acts, compared with *pempō*, which occurs only 80 times, 33 in John and 22 in Luke-Acts. *Pempō* expresses the simple idea of sending, whereas *apostellō* nearly always carries the idea of divine commission. In the Fourth Gospel, Jesus uses *apostellō* to denote divine authority and to ground his own mission in God as the one responsible for Jesus' words and acts (John 3:17; 5:37-38; 6:29, 57; 7:29; 17:3, 8, 21; but occasionally *pempō* substitutes for *apostellō* in the Fourth Gospel). In the New Testament, *apostellō* becomes virtually a theological term for sending forth to serve God with God's own authority. It is closely linked with the power of the name of God.

The term *apostolos* (= "sent one, commissioned envoy") appears 79 times in the New Testament, 29 in the Pauline literature and 34 in Luke-Acts. It designates a person sent with full authority as well as a bearer of the gospel message (cf. Acts 1:26; Matt. 10:2; Mark 6:30; Acts 8: 1). It may on occasion refer to missionaries who were not of the Twelve (Acts 14:4, 14; Gal. 1:19; Rom. 16:7; 1 Cor. 15:7). In one case, Jesus himself is referred to as "the apostle and high priest of our confession" (Heb. 3: 1).

Still another term for "going" and "sending," the Greek intransitive *poreuomai* is frequently identified with sending on a divine mission. Jesus goes to the people (Luke 4:42; Matt. 19:15; Luke 13:33) in a manner that connects his travels with his divine mission. *Poreuomai* also describes the journey of the disciples and apostles to fulfill their gospel mission (Matt. 10:6; 28:19; Acts 8:26; 10:20; 19:21; 22:5). Similarly, *poreuomai* describes Paul's mission to round up Christians before his conversion (Acts 9: 1, 3).

Not every instance of "sending" in the Scriptures is linked to the divine name or authority, but there is a sufficient correlation to suggest that

God as Father, Son, or Spirit is the chief sending agent in biblical revelation, and that prophets, apostles, and other divine messengers are characteristically commissioned to go and to act or speak in the name of God. The evidence points to the fact that sending or going out in mission, and calling upon or declaring the name of God, are intrinsically linked.

In this sense, "naming the name" of Jesus (Acts 4:12) should not be viewed as a singular or isolated event set apart from all other instances of invoking the divine name; it is, rather, a particular expression of invoking Christ's name in the circumstances of public challenge and testimony before the council of the Sanhedrin. Similarly, the Great Commission to make disciples, baptize, and teach in the name of the Trinity (Matt. 28:19) is not a unique, unprecedented, or qualitatively different appeal to divine authority but rather a summary charge given by the Lord to the apostles after the resurrection to continue and complete the apostolic mission on which they were already embarked.

The disciples of Jesus are all called by baptism and sent to bear witness to the name of the Lord at all times and in all circumstances, and to accept whatever consequences might attend their obedient response to that sending. However conditions and circumstances may differ, invoking the name of God and obedience to sending belong to the normal biblical description of Christian life. God continues to send faithful witnesses into the world and desires that the divine name in all its salvific power and meaning be manifested in the world to those who do not know it.

Two Kinds of God-Language

This study is predicated on the assumption that the biblical perspective on divine naming and sending is still relevant to Christian identity and that it continues to play a part in shaping Christian mission, Christian vocation, and the life of Christian community today. How can that relevance be expressed and what are its implications for us?

At this point it will be helpful to make a distinction between two kinds of God-language: "missiological naming" of God and "doxological naming." Both kinds of naming are found in the Bible and also in the Christian community. We may for the moment set aside profane references to God-language as being either irrelevant or as having mainly negative theological significance. What is meant by these two terms?

By *doxological* naming of God we mean the internal language of the Christian community as it invokes the divine name in hymns of praise, liturgy, public worship, confession of faith and creeds, intercession for church and world, catechetical instruction, sermonizing, blessing, and benediction. Doxological language is the language of affirmation of faith and acclamation of God's goodness. In terms of the gathered community it is the language of solidarity, identity, common commitment and discipleship. Because of its inward character and its close relationship to eucharistic worship as the heart of Christian fellowship with Christ, doxological language is unhesitatingly trinitarian, christological, and pneumatological. Within the bosom of the family there is no shame or hesitation about using any and all of the many divine names.

Even a cursory glance at our major liturgical texts will reveal the richness and diversity of names used to honor and glorify God: God in the Highest, Lord God, Heavenly King, Almighty God, Father, Lord Jesus Christ, Son of the Father, Lamb of God, Holy One, Most High, Holy Lord, God of Power and Might, Blessed One, and others. These are all names for God known only to the initiated; they do not belong to the street or the marketplace. They are the internal language of the Christian community used for the glorification of God (doxology) and the edification of the people (*oikodomē*).

With this doxological use of God-language we may contrast *missiological* naming, that is, the external language of the Christian community used in mission and public witness to the world. Missiological naming is God-language stripped of the aura of mystery and reduced to plain fundamentals. It is the language of public declaration of faith, the explanation of the raison d'etre of Christian existence. In the conflict situation of Acts 3–4, it is the repeated naming of "Jesus Christ of Nazareth" as the one source of healing and salvation and the source of Christian boldness. It is uneducated, ordinary people saying, "Whether it is right in the sight of God to listen to you rather than to God, you must judge; for we cannot but speak of what we have seen and heard" (Acts 4:19-20).

In the situation of the Diaspora it is the readiness at all times "to make a defense to any one who calls you to account for the hope that is in you" (1 Peter 3:15). Before Pharaoh, it is the divine imperative to "Let my people go" (Exod. 5:1). To Herod, who wants to kill Jesus, it is the terse message, "Go and tell that fox, . . . I [must] finish my course" (Luke 13:32). In the Little Apocalypse (Mark 13; Matthew 24; Luke 21), it is the witness of believers *in extremis* before governors and kings, given without anxiety or forethought, but prompted by the Holy Spirit. Missiological naming includes the testimony of martyrs: "Lord, do not hold this sin against them" (Acts 7:60).

Missiological God-language is, therefore, not the language of solidarity and affirmation but is often spoken in an atmosphere of controversy or tension. It may be harsh and polemical, as in the condemnation of heresy, unbelief, or unresponsiveness. Or it may be mild, amicable, and temperate, as befits the naming of God's name among those who have never heard it. " 'What must I do to be saved?' 'Believe in the Lord Jesus, and you will be saved, you and your household' " (Acts 16:30-31). In the case of dialogue with people of other living faiths and ideologies, it means naming God's name with reverence and humility and being willing to listen with respect and attentiveness to other names of God mentioned by one's dialogue partners. "What therefore you worship as unknown, this [God] I proclaim to you" (Acts 17:23). In the approach to powers and principalities, it means naming the divine name with confidence and steadfastness, being neither intimidated nor silenced by threat or pressure. "And now I stand here on trial for hope in the promise made by God to our fathers" (Acts 26:6).

Implications for Church and Mission

By way of concluding, let us attempt to summarize some of the major implications of our study of missiological naming—"Who shall I say sent me?"—for the life of the church and its mission in the world.

1. Doxological naming and missiological naming of the name(s) of God are two characteristic expressions of God-language in the Scriptures and in Christian community. The one is internal and refers to the preferred language of the eucharistic community as it gathers at the table of the Lord to be in fellowship with the triune God and with the saints of all times and places. The other is the external language employed by the Christian community, or its appointed representatives, as they represent the church in the world. It is the language of mission and public witness.

2. While Scripture in both the Old and the New Testament presents a rich, diverse, and balanced picture of both types of God-language, the Christian community today appears to express a marked preference for doxological language, the internal language of Christian community. Some consequences of this are that the church's liturgical language, including God-language, is not usually intelligible to outsiders who have not been initiated. Visitors hear a strange language spoken within the walls of the church. Moreover, books about God, normally written in

terms of the in-house jargon of the Christian community for devotees of
theology, are not generally intelligible or attractive to outsiders, even to
serious readers or inquirers. The language of the church's *didachē* echoes
that of its *doxology*.

3. Why is this so? Why is it true that the Christian community feels
more comfortable and more at home with the internal language of the
gathered community than with the kind of communication that would
be required by public or secular discourse? The church encounters little
risk or challenge in using doxological language; doubtless much
strengthening and affirmation are derived from repeated invocation of
the divine name and attributes (*oikodomē*).

Might this also suggest a fear of confrontation on the part of the
church—a fear of casting its pearls before swine or of exposing its precious treasures to the critical inspection of the world? Do Christians fear
that exposure of the Christian "mysteries" to the eyes and ears of the
world would lead to profanation of the divine name, to rejection of the
salvation claims of Jesus Christ, or to the danger that the church as insti-
tution might be condemned as irrelevant or presumptuous?

4. To this we answer that the Christian community—above all,
through its specially commissioned agents—needs to restore the use of
missiological naming (the use of God-language in public discourse) if it is
to fulfill its mission in the world. Areas of special concern are *kerygma* (cf.
Peter's public sermon on the Day of Pentecost, Acts 2:14ff.); *evangelism*;
dialogue (*a*) with people of other faiths, (*b*) with holders of anti-Christian
ideologies, above all with Marxists, secularists, and humanists, and (*c*)
with scientists and technologists; *advocacy* of human rights (cf. Pope
John Paul's numerous appeals before world leaders and the United Nations) and of justice issues; Christian commentary and critique of the
mass media, including television and the cinema. We affirm that risks
must be taken in using God-language and invoking divine authority, but
this is the nature of Christian mission. Without missiological naming, the
church risks becoming irrelevant and denying its calling to be "a light to
the nations."

5. If church representatives wish to engage the world in public discourse and dialogue on the world's "own turf"—that is, on issues that
claim the attention of both church and world—they must learn to speak
the language of the world. Doxological God-language will not serve in
the public forum, the street, or the marketplace. The communication
priorities must be *clarity*, *directness*, and demonstrated *relevance*. The

world does not expect Christians to deny their God or to disavow their faith stance. It does, however, expect Christians to speak with the clarity and forthrightness of the prophet Nathan, who declared to King David, "Thou art the man!" (2 Sam. 12:7) without hemming, hawing, or beating about the bushes. For the world does not need pious religiosity so much as sound counsel based on careful reflection on the prophetic and apostolic Scriptures. The world will listen when the church has a relevant and divinely inspired word to speak. It may reject that word and jail the messenger, but at least it will take the word seriously. But it will pay no heed if it suspects that the messenger's word is phony.

9

Jay C. Rochelle

DOXOLOGY AND
THE TRINITY

*T*he task I chose has four parts. First, we will establish what we mean by doxology. Second, we will consider the consequences of what we find as a definition of doxology. Third, we will consider the chief doxology of the church as found in the eucharistic prayer. Lastly, we will extrapolate some directions as a result of our study.

Defining Doxology

Doxology means at root the use of language to praise God. What kind of language gives praise? Are there forms of language especially geared to making praise, or are the forms made special by their use?

We may answer the first half of that question with a no. Any and all forms of language are theoretically acceptable and usable for doxology, including those beyond the realm of sensible speech (glossolalia and liturgical interjections such as Alleluia, Hosanna, and Maranatha); at the same time, there is a poetic appearance to most doxology. Often forms will exhibit meter, rhythm, and in some cases rhyme. Classic examples are the Magnificat and the Benedictus, the Benedictus qui venit, the Christ hymn at Phil. 2:5-11 (*Lutheran Book of Worship*, canticle 20), the Te Deum of the West and the cherubic hymn of the East. Such poetic hymns echo earlier liturgical models in Jewish tradition, especially of course the psalms.

We may, at the same time, answer the second half of the question with a yes. Forms of speech do appear special by their use in the doxology of the church. This may be due simply to the religious patina with which people invest them and not through any inherent quality in the

form itself. However, we may safely maintain that liturgical language is
poetic. As Gail Ramshaw has said: "The vocabulary and the grammar of
worship have at their root the multivalence and ambiguity with which
our age seems uneasy. . . . It is not only certain aspects of liturgy which
are poetry. Rather it is the rite as a whole which is an extended poem. We
need not be surprised when social anthropologists tell us that ritual action is metaphor."[1]

Poetic form is thus not necessarily the exclusive realm of doxology,
although it is customary. The reason for the extensive use of poetic form,
as we may conclude from Ramshaw's argument among others, is to be lo-
cated not in aesthetics but in theology.[2]

Since Christianity is a theistic religion, that is, God is envisioned to
ex-ist, to stand apart (even as Ground of Being) from humanity, the Deity
must be addressed in personal terms; there is no alternative to this unless we are prepared to give up the personalistic quality of our theism.

Since we are drawn to this form of personal address, because Deity
is at once transcendent and wholly other while immanent and incarnational in Christian understanding, we have no choice but to use what
David Tracy calls the analogical imagination to name God, in which case
we are landed in the territory of simile, metaphor, and story; this is the
domain of poetry.[3] Hence the peculiar incarnational theism of our tradition forces us to use forms of language that are poetic in that they are
metaphorical and/or analagous. God is not a rock; but we can use that
analogy to indicate qualities we associate with Deity, for example,
strength, steadfastness, solidity, and shelter ("Rock of Ages, Cleft for Me"
was written as a poetic reflection on the thirty-second chapter of Exodus
and one particular cliff face on the east coast of England).

Doxology does not so much answer questions as assert that there is
One to praise. We affirm, with Dietrich Bonhoeffer, that Christians have
no immediate knowledge of God, that Christ is the mediator of all our
knowledge of God, the means through whom we know God,[4] and that
such knowledge of God is mediated both by specific "historical" events
(miracles, passion, resurrection) and in speech actions in our time which
bear a promise of the presence of Christ (actions in ritual time). We recall
that this knowledge is built on faith; that is, it is a hope to which we freely
and voluntarily cleave and which leads us to assert that *some* historical
events and *some* ritual events are more important than others in disclos-
ing the presence of holiness in the world. Sacramental theology always,

in some way, safeguards this by the caveat that the true meaning of sacramental grace is known only by and to the eye of the faith.[5]

In this search for analogies that enable us to understand God, then, we hold certain models and paradigms central for our faith. In Christian faith, these models and paradigms grow out of and relate back to the biblical witness, and therefore personal experience is both judged by and correlated to the biblical models, not the other way around. We hereby affirm that beyond and behind the witness of the Bible and the church's history stands a universal experience of the holy.

Doxology is possible only if there is One to praise, in other words. Doxology makes no sense unless that One is personal, more than the projection or introjection of psychic phenomena. We cannot praise or thank unless there is One who can receive thanks and praise. In recent years, more and more attention has been placed on the meaning of the eucharist as thanksgiving, its place in the berakah and hodayot tradition, and an entire theology has been written that takes as its starting point the principle of thanksgiving.[6]

If Christian liturgy is but one dramatic-ritual structure to express a reality that is only psychological or mentally known, then it ought not continue. For then we would simply be using liturgy to remind ourselves of an inherent truth we may know by intuition or experience, apart from revelation.

At the heart and center of our Christian praise is the impact of the resurrection. The engine for our praise is the proclamation of the risen Christ. God in Christ offers new life to the faithful in the power of the Holy Spirit, and such new life must come from outside human experience through both proclamation and enactment since resurrection is not a word we can proclaim unto ourselves. The message of resurrection always breaks in upon us as a foreign word, an alien word, but a word that brings life and hope and enables forgiveness.

Let us turn now to the historic understanding of doxology. We find that the term has been narrowly interpreted to refer to the following:

1. The hymn Gloria in Excelsis is the "greater doxology." This hymn is connected biblically with the incarnation in Luke's Gospel (2:14). It praises God for bringing peace to earth; in it, we specifically "worship," "give thanks," and "praise" (doxologize) God for God's "glory" (*doxa*).

2. The hymn Gloria Patria is the "lesser doxology." It also is trinitarian in form and has been used as a conclusion to the psalms to locate them in a new covenant understanding of God; this doxology is early in

church use and figures in the christological controversies of the third and fourth centuries; it is in evidence already in the writings of Origen, and its current form dates from the end of the fourth century (we should note well that this doxology was in use in the second century *apart from* the later christological issues it is connected with).[7]

3. The conclusion to the Lord's Prayer ("For the kingdom, the power, and the glory are yours now and forever") is called its doxology.

4. The full termination of the prayer of the day, "through your Son, Jesus Christ our Lord, who lives and reigns with you and the Holy Spirit . . . " is known as a doxology. This ancient conclusion, as Josef Jungmann states, "is not concerned with the *coming down* of the gifts but with the *going up* of our prayer. Our prayer should come to God through Christ who, as our representative, as our head, as our High Priest, is already with God. Christ is, so to speak, the bridge over which our prayer can reach God."[8]

5. The conclusion to a eucharistic prayer ("through him, with him, in him, in the unity of the Holy Spirit, all honor and glory . . . ") is called its doxology.

6. Some hymns have a concluding stanza that ascribes glory to the Holy Trinity (see, e.g., *Lutheran Book of Worship* 253, 267, 269, 275 et passim), which is called a doxology.

7. Any ascription of praise to the Holy Trinity is called a doxology. Thus, we may distinguish between doxological language, the language of common praise, and doxologies per se: at least historically, the latter term has, with the singular exception of the conclusion to the Lord's Prayer, been reserved for forms that are trinitarian in structure.

To say this, however, might be somewhat misleading if we took it to mean that doxology and doctrinal language were one and the same simply because doxologies have been historically trinitarian. Doxological language, even in trinitarian form, is not language that talks *about* God so much as it is language that gives praise *to* God. The critical function of theology is momentarily suspended when the community is at prayer and praise, although theology reflects critically on doxological statements.

In worship, the community does not refer to a doctrine of God but directly to God; it does not speak about God or about the existence of God. All such questions are set aside and simple response is made to the revelation of God as it is understood within the community. The language does not discuss the extent to which it is possible to speak about

God; it does not discuss the conditions under which such speech is possible, nor does it dictate the form of such discourse. In prayer, God is addressed; in preaching God is proclaimed.

The aim of doxology is not to render ancient texts relevant to the person of today so much as it is to render each today relevant to the One who is lauded in such words, who is in reality the fulfillment of each now and here of our personal and corporate being. Doxology fits the moment into an eternal context, fits the place into infinity. We incise crosses on the altar in the four corners and in the center to state that the word event which occurs on this mensa is the crossing point of time and eternity; for the moment of use, the altar represents the still point of the turning world. This is a mark of doxology.

Doxology is directed beyond itself and thus is not, strictly speaking, descriptive or evaluative language. It is invocative and evocative; doxology calls into consciousness an experienced reality by a name that has an identifiable historic meaning. The trinitarian name is thus the name of an experience, not of a thing. When it becomes the name of a thing it has ceased to invoke reality.

Doxology bears its own justification; praise has its own raison d'etre, precisely because it is not self-referential. Praise, by its very nature, is directed away from the praise giver to a something or someone who is worthy of praise (namely, the root of worship, "worthship") and whose existence is perceived to be, in some way, healthful and health-giving to the praise giver. Praise is by nature ecstatic.

The Trinitarian Shape of Doxology

We should note, at least in passing, that the trinitarian shape of doxology means, in Christian perspective, that genuine praise can achieve corporate verbal expression. Christianity places some faith in the ability to praise God correctly, that is, to achieve ortho-doxy. Christian worship is opulent and redolent with imagery of and for both the mouth and the eye.[9]

At the same time, as Geoffrey Wainwright points out, "It is the Christian community that transmits the vision which the theologian, as an individual human being, has seen and beleived. As a believer, the theologian is committed to serving the Christian community in the transmission and spread of the vision among humanity. Worship is the place in which that vision comes to a sharp focus, a concentrated expression, and it is here that the vision has often been found to be at its most appealing."[10]

The doxologies of the church proceed from a biblical understanding of the experience of the Holy. This does not mean that other understandings are rejected; if the principal experience of the Holy is a mystery that attracts and repels at the same time, this means that our experience is rooted in an awareness of coincidence of opposites. In the history of the church, this awareness of the coincidence of opposites is expressed through that *story* of the ways by which persons in past times have experienced this Holy One and through what "persons" the Holy has sounded. Put simply, if you want to know who God is, you ask about what God has done. In the Bible, God is eternally the One who saved Israel at the exodus and God is eternally the One who raised Jesus from the dead. The biblical witness, in other words, is shaped in such a way that the transcendent Holy Other is experienced simultaneously as the immanent Personal Lover in and through the Trinity. God is both lawgiver and graceful love at the same time. Law and Gospel coinhere; they arise mutually in our experience. Where this mutual or paradoxical recognition occurs, to my mind at least, this is where doxology arises naturally.

Therefore, in the corporate worship of the church, we consider proper and ordinary that naming of God which takes place in conscious memorial of the biblical witness to the One whom Jesus called Father, to Jesus himself, who is confessed as the *kyrios* and the Christ (Romans 10 and 1 John 4), and to the Spirit, who is present at creation (Genesis 1) and at incarnation (John 1) and who testifies to the truth of Jesus' mission (John 14–16).

The Christian community is a community of memory. Our hope is built on memory, specifically the memory of Christ's death and the hope of the Parousia.[11] Christian liturgy has, historically, reminded us that we live out of Christ's death (the covenantal act by which we see ourselves engrafted into the people of God, Romans 6) and offers us a "foretaste" or down payment of the feast to come (Revelation 4).

The biblical understanding of God that we celebrate in the corporate doxologies of the church does not undercut the witness of the Hebrew Scriptures to the one God, the Holy One of Israel, but builds upon it in such a way that Christians might achieve a self-understanding as heirs of Israel and persons engrafted onto the stock of Israel (both Pauline images). Christians, regardless of the details of their separation from Judaism sometime before the second Jewish Revolt (132–35 C.E.), knew themselves related to the Holy One through Jesus. Only in perverse times does naming the Trinity stand as a barrier to our solidarity with the Jews.[12]

That the historic doxologies are trinitarian underscores three thruths about the shape of our worship:[13]

First, the shape of our worship is *theoultimate*. All of our praise is ultimately directed to *theos*, whom we know as the God of the covenant with Israel and with us through the witness and power of the resurrection.

Second, the shape of our worship is *christocentric* in that our approach to the *theos* is made through the One whom we confess as the Christ; our solidarity with Judaism is expressed in this point. We confess through our christocentricity that we cannot gain access to the One who is in covenant with Israel except through the One whom we confess to be the Messiah sent to Israel—even if Israel does not confess him as such. (This is a quandary worthy of further study, though not here.) Several things are clear about this christocentrism, however. First, the messianic mission of Jesus in peacemaking and love has constructive power to unite people in the worship of the Holy One and in service of others; and second, acknowledging Jesus as *kyrios* gives a critical posture over against the state, which may be in the clutches of the demonic aspects of the principalities and powers. In one of the various atonement models of the New Testament, Jesus rises triumphant over such principalities and powers (Colossians 1–2).

Third, the shape of our worship is *pneumatagogic*. That is to say, we are led by the Spirit into confession of the one God known in three persons. This latter point has not been fully emphasized in the Western church; we have much to learn from our Christian brothers and sisters of the Orthodox concerning the activity of the Holy Spirit. Here is one Orthodox understanding: "[The Spirit] is the very breath which carries language, which enables us to hear it and to receive it as a living seed in the soil of our hearts. Each time we attempt to speak of the Spirit we fail miserably to grasp the wind, the breath that is the very principle of all speech. . . . I would retain from St. Basil the idea that the spirit is the very place both of adoration and sanctification, the power of prayer in us, the longing for the Father, the revealer of Christ's lordship. . . . The language of praise appears as the most adequate to the mystery of the Spirit, for he is the inspirer and author of genuine prayer in our hearts."[14]

That the historic doxologies of the church are trinitarian means that the corporate worship and devotion of the church is intimately related to the public faith of the church. This is, as we recall, the principle *lex orandi, lex credendi*; or "praying shapes believing." This is an important balance in the life of the church. Only with fear and trepidation has this order been reversed in the history of the church; it was so reversed in the time of the Reformation. "It is a matter of plain history that there has been a 'catholic' tendency to let liturgical and devotional practice lead in the 'development' of doctrine, although the magisterium has maintained a right of control. On the other hand, the critical principle of 'protestantism' has sought to bring both worship and dogma to a doctrinal bar that is more directly scriptural."[15] Under duress the Reformers felt that they had to strip away accretions to the liturgy on the basis of a renwed understanding of the church's faith.

If orthodoxy means "right praise," then a certain watchfulness over the forms of liturgy is necessary; at the same time, in order not to squelch the movement and flow of the Spirit in the church, we may not prematurely cut off innovations. We are involved in a constant search for balance.

That the historic doxologies are trinitarian means that they are intimately connected to the name into which we are baptized. Gerard Sloyan has shown that the Apostles' Creed grew "like Topsy, not in response to heretical denials of the faith but as a process of summary catechetical affirmations. Like all creedal formularies it is an exercise in self-identity, corporate Christian affirmation." Lest this be misunderstood, he later goes on emphatically to state, in reference to both the Apostles' Creed and the Nicene Creed, "As to content, while [these] creed(s) seem to know a great deal about God and the work of God among us, it is the property of a church which maintains that what we do not know about God is infinitely more than what we do know.[16]

The Apostles' Creed originated in a catechetical (question-and-answer) form. Here we have a ritual process that shapes believing. As we said above, the Holy Trinity is an experience and must not be allowed to degenerate into a thing. Those who underwent the catechetical process knew that they were to be baptized into the name (or ownership) of the Holy Trinity. They confessed the name at baptism to identify with the body of Christ in that place, to identify with the God of Israel made known and interpreted through the church's faith in the resurrection, to identify with the meaning of Jesus as Christ and *kyrios*, the latter term in particular imbued with political importance, and to identify with the Holy Spirit as the One who brings us into the truth and gives us the gift of discernment through our faith in Christ, a discernment ratified in our baptism. The event of repentance–catechesis–baptism–chrismation–first communion was the way the confession of the name was made, and name makes sense chiefly within the framework of that experience of entry into the faith.[17]

This catechetical process enabled unity in the faith. Ignatius of Antioch had suggested that the function of *episcopē* was to attest and guarantee the unity of the church, a unity enabled through the shaping of faith by *didachē* (teaching) that the church might be united in *doxa*.[18]

Relating the Eucharistic Prayer to Praise

The eucharistic prayers grow from Jewish roots. In Jewish prayer life, the eighteen benedictions (so called because they traditionally begin with the word *berakah*: *"Blessed* are you, O Lord our God, Ruler of the Universe")* contain at their heart six blessing prayers which praise and give thanks for creation, for redemption, and for revelation. "Throughout the [Jewish] liturgy, we find repeatedly juxtaposed the three basic and complementary motifs of Creation–Revelation (viz. the Giving of the Torah)–Redemption, which in the Rabbinic world-view mark respectively the beginning of the history of mankind, the critical turning-point in the progression of that history, and the ultimate goal and final destination of the historic continuum."[19]

But more goes on here than Christian adaptation of the berakah prayers. For the form commonly used in third person address to thank God (hodayot) is mixed with the berakah.[20] Now, this verb is complex in usage; it means not only to give thanks but also to make confession, which would be rendered in Greek by *exomologemai* but is consistently rendered by *eucharistein*, in the sense of making a sacrifice of thanksgiving or praise.

As the eucharistic prayer develops over time, it picks up these themes (as do certain of the holidays: e.g., Pentecost, which in Jewish use is connected with the giving of the Torah, shifts in Christian adaptation to commemorate the giving of the Spirit).[21] The Creator is thanked—and is also addressed as Father through the invitation of Christ. For example, in the *Dialogue with Trypho*, chap. 117, we read, "There is not a single race of humans . . . among whom prayers and thanksgivings are not offered to the Father, the Creator of the Universe, in the name of the crucified Jesus."[22]

The Redeemer is remembered (which is to say, proclaimed to the Christian assembly as crucified and risen Lord, almost invariably with the note that he entered *voluntarily* into suffering; i.e., "handed over to a death he freely accepted," from the *Apostolic Tradition* of Hippolytus [ca. 215 C.E.?]. The Spirit—who is Revealer as well as Sanctifier—is invoked upon the assembly and the gifts. In the anaphora of Addeus and Maris (ca. 200 C.E.), the assembly prays, "May your Holy Spirit come and rest, Lord, on this, the offering your servants make you. May he bless and sanctify it, that through it we may receive forgiveness of our sins and pardon for our offenses, confident hope of rising from the dead, and a new life in the kingdom of heaven with all who have ever pleased you."[23] The eucharistic prayer is thus trinitarian in shape from early times and the prayer originates in praise; it identifies our access, as Christians, to God through Christ in the power of the Spirit.

At the same time, as Robert Ledogar has pointed out, we cannot avoid the doctrinal relationship of doxology; "public praise is a statement of what I believe in."[24] Joseph Sittler said it simply: "Liturgy is prayed dogma."[25] "This kind of praise is an act of faith—if you understand faith as basically a commitment rather than an intellectual assent. It is a confession. Just as the early creeds were called confession, so were acts of praise."[26]

The earliest eucharistic prayer outside scriptural references is that of the *Didache*, and early second-century Syrian writing. The prayer does not yet make specific reference to the Holy Spirit; only the "food and drink" are referred to as *pneumatikos*. The community is explicitly prohibited from allowing anyone at the eucharist who has not been baptized in the name of the *kyrios*.[27]

By the time of Justin Martyr's *First Apology* (ca. 150 C.E.), we find this reference to the offertory at the eucharist: "We bless [eulogize] the Maker of all things through his Son Jesus Christ and through the Holy Spirit over all that we receive."[28] Henceforth this formula, with slight variations, becomes central to Christian praying.

We refrain from further recitation of the history of the prayer. The point is clear: already in the early church, the heart of the eucharistic prayer is rooted in Jewish ritual, and enables us to thank and praise the Creator/Father who has been made known to the nations by Jesus/Christ/Lord/Son, in and through the power of the Holy Spirit.[29]

Future Directions

Ambrose well wrote, *Quod confiteor lingua teneat adfectus,* or roughly, "What the tongue confesses the heart addresses."[30] The trinitarian shape of praise has perdured because the Holy Trinity has been taught in liturgical catechesis, which channels our vision of God; we are committed to the name of the Holy Trinity in the covenant of baptism. At every turn in our corporate liturgy we are reminded of the name in whose glory we assemble and whose praises we render. Trinitarian faith is sung in creed and hymn, outlined each week in the eucharistic prayer, and related to daily prayer.

But certain factors inhibit this holistic notion of praise. Here are a few of those factors:

1. As far as I can tell, the restive nature of many parishoners at worship stems partly from a poor background in the meaning of worship and partly from the slipshod approach to liturgy often taken in parishes, where liturgy is treated as a fragmentary collection of antiquarian delights and not as a whole cloth. Only now do we begin again to draw links between pastoral care and ritual to deepen faith by expanding people's imagery for God and by applying such imagery as a healing tool in life situations.[31] We seek to understand how praise and healing are related.

2. A powerful kind of literalism is afoot. The wanton application of feminine pronouns for God can be as much a mistake as simply clinging, in a reactionary manner, to solely masculine ones. We are caught between a rock and a hard place. We can no longer communicate in English that God transcends gender differences by the use of the male pronouns, because they have become gender specific in American usage. All right. We have problems, however, if we call God and Jesus "he" and call the Holy Spirit "she." Such splitting of genders between persons of the Trinity serves only to make mischief; it cannot be done without creating faulty, impoverished understanding. Obviously the feminine needs to be included in Deity, as does the masculine, but we must remember that such attempts are inclusive of human nature and not definitive for divine nature. We are in a period of experimentation in which no one has *the* answer.

3. We should note contemporary shifts in consciousness as represented, for example, by the revolution in physics in the twentieth century, much of which revolution seems better grasped through a Buddhist

world view than through a Christian one, since the Buddhist view, in common contemporary physics, also understands that the psychic action within an observer is capable of changing the process under observation. In such a shifted view, the Christian concept of a "creator" who stands wholly outside the natural processes needs revision. So will the forms of praise that arise on the basis of this paradigm shift.

4. There is also the intrapsychic search for wholeness, particularly in terms of addressing the feminine and masculine sides of oneself. Listen to the celebrated Canadian author Robertson Davies as he writes in his masterful novel *What's Bred in the Bone*. The hero, Francis Cornish, is now a teenager discovering his sexuality. In Davies' novel, there is an off-stage interchange between the "biographer angel" and the muse, or daimon, throughout the story. The daimon speaks:

> Of course, . . . he was looking for The girl, the girl deep in himself, the feminine ideal that has some sort of existence in every man of any substance, and my Francis was a man of substance. It wasn't effeminacy, which is what anybody who discovered him would have supposed. It certainly wasn't homosexuality, for Francis never had more than the usual dash of that. He was groping for the Mystical Marriage, the unity of the masculine and the feminine in himself, without which he would have been useless in his future life as an artist and as a man who understood art. *Useless as any sort of man — rich man, poor man, beggar man, thief; not to speak of tinker, tailor, soldier, sailor—who is destined to see more than a few inches beyond the end of his nose.* This was the beginning of the search for the Mystical Marriage, which is one of the great quests, and as usual the quest was longer and more important than the eventual discovery.[32]

We are on ground that has been well trod throughout the ages as people grope toward wholeness and give praise where they find it in bits and pieces. The wholeness of God is offered us that we might come to wholeness, which involves coming to terms with our masculine and feminine aspects within. In Christian terms, the *doxa* we offer is related to the *doxa* we have received.

Help from the East

"Now the Lord is the Spirit; and where the Spirit of the Lord is, there is liberty. But we all, with unveiled face, beholding as in a mirror the glory of the Lord, are being transformed into the same image from glory to glory, just as by the Spirit of the Lord" (2 Cor. 3:17-18). This startling passage is at the heart of the spirituality of the Christian East. Gregory of Nyssa[33] was a key formulator of this spirituality in early centuries; for him, sin was the refusal to grow, to become a full human being (Irenaeus it was who said that the glory of God is a human being fully realized), and the process of growth is perpetual throughout life; since the glory and majesty of God's presence in a life are ever new, there can be no point of satiety. Thus we are being transformed from glory to glory.[34]

Those who are pilgrims in the Christian way see with veiled face, but nonetheless really and truly, the glory of God. Metropolitan Philaret of Moscow (1782–1867) says: "God the Father is the 'Father of Glory' (Eph. 1:17); the Son of God is the 'brightness of his glory' (Heb. 1:3) and . . . so too the Spirit of God is the 'Spirit of glory' (1 Pet. 4:14). God lives in this glory. . . . He gives His glory to those whom He allows to participate in it and receive it; it then returns again to Him. This eternal circulation of the Divine Glory, as it were, constitutes the blessed life, the happiness of creatures."[35] Thus it is participation in the glory of God which is marked by the participation of the believer in the divine liturgy.

Pseudo-Macarius (mid-fourth to mid-fifth century, actual identity unknown) writes, "Whoever approaches God and truly desires to be a partner of Christ must approach with a view to this goal, namely, to be changed and transformed from his former state and attitude and become a good and new person, harboring nothing of the 'old man' (2 Cor. 5:17). . . . For indeed our Lord Jesus Christ came for this reason, to change and to transform and renew human nature and to recreate this soul that had been overturned by passions through the transgression."[36]

For the Christian East, participation in divine liturgy *is* life in the *doxa* of God, and this participation gradually leads to transformation of the life of the believer. Thus all forms of praise are bound up in liturgy, because in Eastern reckoning there can really be no praise outside that framework. Insofar as we in the West are able, we need to breathe this spirit in our worship to learn how to incorporate these new psychic and physical understandings, for we will see the search for the Mystical Marriage (Davies) and the interplay of all creation as capable of being both addressed and expressed through playful forms of praise whose end is the Holy Trinity.

The eucharistic prayer creates the framework for praise. The eucharist is central to the church's praise, and the eucharistic prayer is central to the celebration. All other forms of praise are subsumed under the praise of the Holy Trinity, but within that framework we pray that God "would cause all useful arts to flourish among us." Therefore a variety of gifts and arts will be manifest among us and useful to the whole celebrative life of worship. Dance, drama, visual arts, and song all play a role in praise-making.

Within the church's eucharist we may in fact locate forms often not thought of as praise, for example, the *intercessions* (now dislocated from the eucharistic prayer to a preceding point) which are understood as the right of the assembly since Christ is our intercessor. Here prayer on behalf of others is understood as a form of praise.[37]

The *eschatological dimension* of the eucharist was lost already by the sixth century in the Western church, a period during which congregational participation in the reception of the elements of holy communion also recedes. The two are interrelated facts of history.[38] In our time, the eschatological dimension is slowly being recaptured, under the impetus of twentieth-century biblical study since the time of Albert Schweitzer's study *The Quest of the Historical Jesus*,[39] the liturgical study of Gregory Dix,[40] and even the controversial work of Odo Casel;[41] and this is now reflected in the World Council of Churches' document *Baptism, Eucharist and Ministry* and the responses to it.[42] This document states: "The eucharist opens up the vision of the divine rule which has been promised as the final renewal of creation, and is a foretaste of it. . . . As it is entirely the gift of God, the eucharist brings into the present age a new reality which transforms Christians into the image of Christ and therefore makes them his effective witnesses."[43] *Baptism, Eucharist and Ministry* ties the eschatological dimension, the inbreaking of the "new reality," to the *mission* of the church: "As it becomes one people, sharing the meal of the one Lord, the eucharistic assembly must be concerned for gathering also those who are at present beyond its visible limits, because Christ invited to his feast all for whom he died. Insofar as Christians cannot unite in full fellowship around the same table to eat the same loaf and drink from the same cup, their missionary witness is weakened at both the individual and the corporate levels."[44]

The mission of the church demands that we recognize the eschatological dimension to all worship. Worship is done in the spirit of the *maranatha* prayer. When we pray *maranatha*, we are ready to be surprised by joy through the newness, the freshness, and the unexpectedness of God's presence. This means that even our forms of language are surrendered to the future vision of the inbreaking reign of God.

No forms of praise will or could prove final. All our praise is provisional and penultimate; all praise will burst forth and spill over as and when the forms become old wineskins. Only the framework of praise for the Holy Trinity remains as the constant, with its center in the memorial, "For as often as we eat this bread and drink this cup, we show forth our Lord's death until he comes" (1 Cor. 11:26).

At the same time, our striving toward eucharistic hospitality demands that praise be shaped so that those who gather may enter into their liturgy and their praise joyfully. This is where I locate the call to move toward inclusive language. When people are frozen out by what is perceived as exclusive language, their praise is curtailed. We do not want to curtail but to encourage praise. Certainly caution is necessary, but curtailment? We might as well try to capture the wind.

Thus, if we wish to expand the community of praise, let us begin with the primal experience of the Holy. Let us invite people to bring into the trinitarian framework all those points in their lives where they believe themselves to have been touched by the Holy. Never mind that we might and will have critical remarks to make about this; the history of the church is the history of criticism of doxology; prayer and belief, in the end, shape each other.

We would do well to reinvent a process of liturgical catechesis within the Protestant tradition, even as our Roman Catholic brothers and sisters have done so well in the Rite of Christian Initiation for Adults. For liturgical catechesis served in the past as a means to channel the raw data of the experience of the Holy into Christian form, and could so serve in our day.

Personal Epilogue: On the Difficulty of Making Praise

The making of praise goes on with or without the kind of analysis and synthesis found in this essay. The making of praise is more important than the making of words about the making of praise. The making of praise is far more interesting than all our analysis of praise, which analysis renders praise null and void. As we said earlier, doxology is rooted in ecstasy, and in order for ecstasy to remain ecstatic we must continue to go out of ourselves in the making of praise.

We gather under the canopy of the Holy Trinity first because our word of praise, our *logion* of *doxa*, is an echo and mirror of the *doxa* which is shared within the Trinity. We are called to speech and song and dance by the Spirit who inspires us to make praise. Those who are richly embedded in and nurtured by resurrection faith hear this call quickening them in many times and places: who can but praise?

We gather under the canopy of the Holy Trinity, under the dome of the historic faith, in order, second, that we have a common language with which to communicate with one another what we have seen and heard in Christ. What some people tell us is that our common language is but a dream; they cannot share our language. These are grave words about the most serious of matters, the difficulty some who want to praise have in making praise in "our" terms. We do well to invite people to share their praise under the canopy and not so quickly to write them off as heretical in intent or belief.

All of us are in search of a pleasing and harmonious balance between the cry of our insistent hearts and the shouting within our souls, on one tray of the scales, and the historic and traditional forms of praise which are given us corporately in the church on the other.

Those who make words for the sake of praise, frankly, often get more grief than those who make praise in other ways. Western Christians, in particular, tend to cling to words as if they were sounder than song, more sure-footed than the dancer, more rooted in the earth than the heavenly song of the harp or the lyre. We tend to believe that words are not so elusive, that they really can capture processes that they name as nouns, when in fact a noun is but the momentary naming of a movement through time and space which happens often enough to become identifiable as a thought, and thus becomes a "thing."

If the fount and source of our praise as well as the aim and end of our praise is the Holy Trinity, however, this should remind us of the elusive nature of our words. For the Holy Trinity can become no such "thing"; the Trinity is our name for the eternal creating by the Father, the eternal begetting of the Son, the eternal procession of the Spirit. These eternals cannot be frozen in time by being rendered as names which then become definitions, for all definitions are limits or boundaries, and the Holy cannot be bound, except through that self-binding we know in the incarnation, which remains eternal mystery. These eternals can only be recognized and worshiped in our time by the making of praise. Hence doxology, ironically, becomes both our means to give praise and our means of escape from that "orthodoxy" which would cramp and strangle all expressions of the Holy Spirit in the human spirit. In making praise we render up the very best that is within us, and all that is within us, in the hope and the faith that the blessed Holy Trinity is both source and ending of our whole life and receives our whole life as an act of praise.

The musician offers melody, and sometimes poetic text with that melody, but it is the melody which is the praise. When Paul Manz plays one of his own hymn tunes, the music is praise, regardless of the words which the music accompanies. When Mark Bangert directs Advent choral vespers, the complete and total sound of voices and instruments in harmony is the praise.

In preaching, praise comes forth creatively in eucharistic liturgy; for to proclaim is also to craft praise as a wizard with words. Preachers speak a word that gathers up the congregation's self-understanding and they present that self-understanding as praise before the Holy One. We speak words to the congregation which evolve and take form out of the biblical witness to the experience of God, in the hope that we will bridge the gap between text and hearer so that the experience which the text reports may be known and may evoke praise in and from the hearers. In preaching, that raw "religious experience" of the Holy is interpreted under the sign of the Trinity. May not the act of preaching be understood as an evocation of the Holy Trinity in the presence of the congregation? And is it not the case that we sing hymnody and speak creed as praise in response to the audible Word?

Liturgy is not merely text and, even so, praise is not merely words. It is more than the words; praise is in the gesture, in the physical elements of water and oil and bread and wine and touch. In the context of the eucharist as the chief and highest praise the church makes, each part plays an important role in the total symphony of praise (cf. Col. 1:27; 3:12-13).

NOTES

1. Introduction: Naming the Name

1. Sallie McFague, *Metaphorical Theology: Models of God in Religious Language* (Philadelphia: Fortress Press, 1982), 1.

2. Walther von Loewenich, *Luther's Theology of the Cross,* trans. J. A. Bouman (Minneapolis: Augsburg Publishing House, 1976), 18.

3. Martin Luther, *Werke,* Kritische Gesamtausgabe, Weimarer Ausgabe (Weimar: Boehlau, 1883 to the present), 40.II:329. I am indebted to my colleague Kurt Hendel for this quotation taken from his response to my chapter in this volume.

4. Ibid., 40.III:337. This quotation also comes from Kurt Hendel's response to my chapter, which focused on Luther's insights on the topic of God-language.

2. The Problem of God-Language Today

1. Naomi Goldenberg, *Changing of the Gods* (Boston: Beacon Press, 1979).

2. Theodore W. Jennings, *Beyond Theism: A Grammar of God-Language* (New York: Oxford University Press, 1985).

3. Gerhard Ebeling, "Existence Between God and God," in *God and Christ: Existence and Province,* Journal for Theology and the Church, 5, ed. Robert W. Funk in association with Gerhard Ebeling) (New York: Harper & Row, 1968), 149.

4. Paul van Buren, *The Secular Meaning of the Gospel* (New York: Macmillan Company, 1963), 103.

5. John A. T. Robinson, *Honest to God* (London: SCM Press; Philadelphia: Westminster Press, 1963), 127.

6. Norman L. Geisler, *Philosophy of Religion* (Grand Rapids: Zondervan Publishing House, 1974), 239. He offers a number of similar quotations from Plotinus's *Enneads.*

7. Paul Tillich, *The Courage to Be* (New Haven: Yale University Press, 1952), 40.

8. See Gustaf Aulén, *The Drama and the Symbols: A Book on Images of God and the Problems They Raise,* trans. Sydney Linton (Philadelphia: Fortress Press, 1970), 90.

9. Martin Luther, *The Bondage of the Will,* trans. J. I. Packer and O. R. Johnson (Westwood, N.J.: Fleming H. Revell Co., 1957), 67.

10. Sallie McFague, *Metaphorical Theology: Models of God in Religious Language* (Philadelphia: Fortress Press, 1982), 1.

11. Ibid., 194.

12. Rev. 1:8; 21:6; 22:13.

13. For a very readable summary of these atheistic challenges, see Hans Küng, *Does God Exist?* trans. Edward Quinn (New York: Doubleday & Co., 1978) 189-340.

14. See Thomas J. J. Altizer et. al., *Deconstruction and Theology* (New York: Crossroad, 1982).

15. Carl A. Raschke, "The Deconstruction of God," in *Deconstruction and Theology*, by Altizer, 27-28.

16. Clifford Geertz, *The Interpretation of Cultures* (New York: Basic Books, 1973), "Religion as a Cultural System," 87-125.

17. Ludwig Wittgenstein, *Philosophical Investigations*, 3d ed. trans. G. E. M. Anscombe (Oxford: Basil Blackwell, 1967).

18. Schubert Ogden, *The Reality of God and Other Essays* (New York: Harper & Row, 1966), 56-57.

19. Eberhard Jüngel, *God as the Mystery of the World*, trans. Darrell L. Guder (Grand Rapids: Wm. B. Eerdmans Publishing Co., 1983), viii.

20. George A. Lindbeck, *The Nature of Doctrine* (Philadelphia: Westminster Press, 1984).

21. Cf. Ronald F. Thiemann, *Revelation and Theology: The Gospel as Narrated Promise* (Notre Dame, Ind.: University of Notre Dame Press, 1985).

22. John Macquarrie, *Principles of Christian Theology* (New York: Charles Scribner's Sons, 1966). I adopted this expression of "a new style natural theology" from Macquarrie and developed it further in my book *The Future of God* (New York: Harper & Row, 1969).

23. Peter Berger, *A Rumor of Angels* (Garden City, N.Y.: Doubleday & Co., 1969), 90.

24. Wolfhart Pannenberg, *Anthropology in Theological Perspective*, trans. Matthew J. O'Connell (Philadelphia: Westminster Press, 1985).

25. Thomas J. J. Altizer, "The Anonymity of God," in *Is God God?* ed. Axel D. Steuer and James Wm. McClendon, Jr. (Nashville: Abingdon Press, 1981), 17-35.

26. Quoted by Ebeling, "Existence Between God and God," in *God and Christ*, ed. Funk, 151.

27. Jennings, *Beyond Theism*, 125.

28. Paul Tillich, *Systematic Theology*, 3 vols. (Chicago: University of Chicago Press, 1951-63), 2:27.

29. Langdon Gilkey, *Naming the Whirlwind: The Renewal of God Language* (Indianapolis: Bobbs-Merrill Co., 1969), 20.

30. Frederick Ferré, *Language, Logic and God* (New York: Harper & Brothers, 1961), 160.

31. Sharon D. Welch, *Communities of Resistance and Solidarity: A Feminist Theology of Liberation* (Maryknoll, N.Y.: Orbis Books, 1985), 1.

32. Ibid., 2.

33. Ibid., 7.

34. Richard Rorty, *Philosophy and the Mirror of Nature* (Princeton, N.J.: Princeton University Press, 1979).

35. Sheila Davaney, "Radical Historicity and the Search for Sure Foundations" (unpublished paper), 18.

36. Ibid., 19.

37. David Hume, *Enquiry Concerning Human Understanding* (Indianapolis: Bobbs-Merrill, 1955).

38. Ludwig Wittgenstein, *Tractatus Logico-Philosophicus*, trans. D. F. Pears and B. F. McGuinness (London: Routledge & Kegan Paul, 1961), 6:44.

39. Ibid., 6:45.

40. Ibid., 6:432.

41. Van Buren, *The Secular Meaning of the Gospel*, 84.

42. Quoted by Ebeling, "Existence Between God and God," in *God and Christ*, ed. Funk, 161.

43. Elisabeth Schüssler Fiorenza, *In Memory of Her* (New York: Crossroad, 1983), 34.

44. Ibid., 118.

45. Ibid., 107.

46. Rosemary Radford Ruether, *Sexism and God-Talk* (Boston: Beacon Press, 1983), 165.

47. Mary Daly, *Beyond God the Father* (Boston: Beacon Press, 1973), 19.

48. McFague, *Metaphorical Theology*, 166, 218 n. 51.

49. Paul Ricoeur, *The Symbolism of Evil*, trans. Emerson Buchanan (New York: Harper & Row, 1967), 348.

50. Juan Luis Segundo offered an extended reflection on the christological confession, "Jesus is God," in a public lecture entitled "Is Chalcedon Out of Date?"

51. James Gustafson, *Ethics from a Theocentric Representative* (Chicago: University of Chicago Press, 1981).

52. John Hick, *God Has Many Names* (Philadelphia: Westminster Press, 1980).

53. Paul Knitter, *No Other Name?* (Maryknoll, N.Y.: Orbis Books, 1984).

54. Tom Driver, *Christ in A Changing World* (New York: Crossroad, 1981).

55. Jüngel, *God as the Mystery of the World*; and idem, *The Doctrine of the Trinity* (Grand Rapids: Wm. B. Eerdmans Publishing Co., 1976).

56. Jürgen Moltmann, *The Trinity and the Kindgdom* (New York: Harper & Row, 1981).

57. Robert W. Jenson, *The Triune Identity* (Philadelphia: Fortress Press, 1982).

58. Wolfhart Pannenberg, "Die Subjectivität Gottes und die Trinitätslehre," and "Der Gott der Geschichte," in *Grundfragen systematischer Theologie*, Gesammelte Aufsätze, vol. 2 (Göttingen: Vandenhoeck & Ruprecht, 1980). See also Panneberg's essay, "Problems of a Trinitarian Doctrine of God," *Dialog* 26 (Fall, 1987), 250-57.

59. Karl Rahner, *The Trinity*, trans. J. Donceel (New York: Herder & Herder, 1970).

60. Walter Kasper, *The God of Jesus Christ*, trans. Matthew J. O'Connell (New York: Crossroad, 1984).

61. Dietrich Bionhoeffer, *Letters and Papers from Prison*, ed. Eberhard Bethge and trans. Reginald H. Fuller (New York: Macmillan Co., 1953), 220.

62. Wolfhart Pannenberg, *Basic Questions in Theology*, trans. George H. Kehm (Philadelphia: Fortress Press, 1971), 139.

63. Wolfhart Pannenberg, *Systematische Theologie*, Vol. 1 (Göttingen: Vandenhoek & Ruprecht, 1988).

64. See Carl E. Braaten, "The Question of God and the Trinity," in *Festschrift for William Hordern*, ed. Walter Freitag (Saskatoon, Sask., 1985).

65. Claude Geffre, " 'Father' as the Proper Name of God." in *God as Father?* ed. Johannes-Baptist Metz and Edward Schillebeeckx, Concilium 143, (New York: Seabury Press, 1981), 44.

66. Paul Ricoeur, "La Paternité: Du fantasme au symbole," *Le conflit des interprétations: Essais d'herméneutique* (Paris, 1969), 476.

3. Reticence and Exuberance in Speaking of God

1. American Heritage Dictionary, "construe, v.: To use syntactically ('The noun "fish" can be construed as either singular or plural')." Just so, the experience "world" can be construed either theistically or nontheistically.

2. Paul Tillich, *Biblical Religion and the Search for Ultimate Reality* (Chicago: University of Chicago Press, 1955), 85.

3. Acts 17:27.

4. Rom. 1:19; and cf. the remainder of the passage.

5. Thus: reticence or exuberance.

6. Dietrich Bonhoeffer, *Letters and Paper from Prison,* ed. Eberhard Bethge (Rev. ed., New York: Macmillan Co., 1967), 141-42.

7. Søren Kierkegaard, *Concluding Unscientific Postscript* (Princeton: Princeton University Press, 1944), 245.

8. In a very personal vein, may I say that I miss the "blank" period that used to exist while communicants were going forward to the altar and returning from it. This period could be quite long in the huge congregations in the area where I grew up (eastern Pennsylvania), running typically about two thousand members. Having been instructed at an early age that it was not to be used simply to gaze at the congregants as they passed by, one found that one was left to one's own thoughts, meditations, ruminations, or prayers. If some stimulus was needed, one opened the service book and read over a hymn or a psalm. But now the time is filled with mandatory hymn-singing, which, however edifying, tends to fill the mind with yet other symbols, perhaps scores of them.

9. The count of Jesus' use of the term "Father" in addressing or speaking of God in the several Gospels is as follows, according to Joachim Jeremias: Mark, 4; Luke, 15; Matthew, 42; John, 109. Cf., Jeremias, "Abba," in *Abba: Studien zur neutestamentlichen Theologie und Zeitgeschichte* (Göttingen: Vandenhoeck & Ruprecht, 1966).

10. Robert Hamerton-Kelly, *God the Father: Theology and Patriarchy in the Teaching of Jesus,* Overtures to Biblical Theology (Philadelphia: Fortress Press, 1979).

11. A Christian visitor to synagogue worship today cannot help being struck by the fact that one of the most common appellations for God in the stated prayers is "Our Father, our King." If this were not deeply Jewish, it surely would not be used, since there has been a strong tendency to avoid anything that could be considered of Christian provenance (Judaism's own "dissimilarity criterion").

Solomon Schechter, the great turn of the century rabbi and founder of Jewish Theological Seminary in New York, waxed quite satirical in defending the authenticity of such father-language in Judaism. He asks rhetorically at one point: "Is the Jew taught to confess his sins daily in the following words: 'Forgive us, our Father, for we have sinned; pardon us, our King, for we have transgressed . . .' or is this formula borrowed from a non-Jewish liturgy? Has the Jew ever heard his mother at the bedside of a sick relative, directing prayers to God, and appealing to him as 'the beloved name, the gracious helper, the merciful Father, and the dear God'; or was it some Christian neighbor to whom he was listening?" (Schechter, *Aspects of Rabbinic Theology: Major Concepts of the Talmud* [New York: Macmillan, 1909; reprint, Schocken Books, 1961], 22-23).

12. *American Heritage Dictionary*, "appellative, *n.*: A name or descriptive epithet." (Thus, not *merely* a name.) Cf. "epithet, *n.*: A term used to characterize the nature of a person or thing."

13. There is a passage in one of the Dead Sea Scrolls, from a Thanksgiving Psalm used by the community there, which combines these father and mother images, plus that of foster father, in a remarkable way:

> My father does not know me,
> And in comparison with you my mother has left me.
> But you are the father of all your faithful
> And rejoice over them as a loving mother over her baby,
> And like a foster-father you cherish in your bosom
> all your creatures.

(1QH 9:35ff.; cited by Hamerton-Kelly, *God the Father*, 54.)

4. "Let God Be God": The Theological Necessity of Depatriarchalizing God

1. Lisa Sowle Cahill, *Between the Sexes* (Philadelphia: Fortress Press, 1985), 33.
2. Sandra M. Schneiders, *Women and the Word : The Gender of God in the New Testament* (New York: Paulist Press, 1986), 13.
3. Beverly Wildung Harrison, *Making the Connections* (Boston: Beacon Press, 1985), 31.
4. Ibid., 92.
5. Paul Tillich, *Systematic Theology, 3 vols.* (Chicago: University of Chicago Press, 1951-63), 1:239.
6. Ibid., 240-41.
7. Gen. 1:27; Gal. 3:28.
8. E.g., Leonard Swidler, "Jesus Was a Feminist," *Catholic World* 212 (1971), 177-83.
9. Mary Daly, *Beyond God the Father* (Boston: Beacon Press 1973), 13.
10. Rosemary Radford Ruether, *Sexism and God-talk* (Boston: Beacon Press, 1983), 23.
11. Schneiders, *Women and the Word*, 34.
12. Gerda Lerner, *The Creation of Patriarchy* (New York: Oxford University Press, 1986), 42.
13. Ibid., 211.
14. Ibid., 86.
15. Ibid., 192.
16. Peggy Reeves Sanday, *Female Power and Male Dominance* (Cambridge: Cambridge University Press, 1981), 230.

17. Ibid., 11-12.

18. Elisabeth Moltmann-Wendel, *A Land Flowing with Milk and Honey: Perspectives on Feminist Theology* (New York: Harper & Row, 1986), 55.

19. Patricia Wilson-Kastner, *Faith, Feminism, and the Christ* (Philadelphia: Fortress Press, 1983).

20. Susan Brooks Thistlethwaite, *Metaphors for the Contemporary Church* (New York: Pilgrim Press, 1983), 112.

21. Isabel Carter Heyward, *Our Passion for Justice, Images of Power, Sexuality, and Liberation* (New York, Pilgrim Press, 1984), 244-45.

22. Ibid., 245.

23. Isabel Carter Heyward, *The Redemption of God: A Theology of Mutual Relation* (Washington, D.C.: University Press of America, 1982), 7.

24. Ibid., 116.

25. Luke 11:27-28.

26. Heyward, *The Redemption of God*, 212.

5. How Israel Conceived of and Addressed God

1. W. Gunther Plaut, *The Torah: A Modern Commentary* (New York: Union of American Hebrew Congregations, 1981), 543.

2. El Shaddai occurs of course also in Gen. 43:14 and 49:25. But is that name for God enough evidence alone for calling these texts Priestly?

3. Marvin H. Pope, *Job*, Anchor Bible (Garden City, N.Y.: Doubleday & Co., 1965), 44. It is noteworthy that in 1 Kings 20:28 Yahweh is being described as an "Elohim of the mountains."

4. Norman C. Habel, *The Book of Job*, Old Testament Library (Philadelphia: Westminister Press, 1985), 135. He observes, "Job and his friends are exploring the nature of God as though he were the Shaddai the fathers knew before the day of Moses (Ex. 6:2-3)."

5. Klaus Koch, "Shaddaj: Zum Verhältnis zwischen israelitischer Monolatrie and nordwestsemitischem Polytheismus," *Vetus Testamentum* 26 (1976): 316.

6. Bernhard Lang, "Die Jahwe-allein-Bewegung," in *Die Geburt des biblischen Monotheismus*, ed. Bernhard Lang (Munich: Kösel-Verlag, 1981), 79.

7. The reader is owed an explanation for the deliberate use of the terms "patriarch" and "fathers" in this text. They are not chosen carelessly. Instead, in full awareness of the matriarchs' historical role, and also of what it must have been even when it was not mentioned in the texts, these words are employed as technical terms, reflecting the texts themselves. These words nevertheless remind us, and tacitly admit, that the biblical references to god(s) of the ancestors mention only males. We never read of the god of any mother, of, e.g., Sarah or Rebecca or Rachel or Leah.

8. Albrecht Alt, *Der Gott der Väter* (1929); in *Kleine Schriften zur Geschichte des Volkes Israel* (Munich: C. H. Beck, 1953), 67/68.

9. It is noteworthy, and has remained a puzzle, that the term for God in the Yahwist's creation story is Yahweh Elohim, not just Yahweh. Yahweh Elohim is hardly found outside of Genesis 2–3. See Claus Westermann, *Genesis 1–11: A*

Commentary (Minneapolis, Augsburg Publishing House, 1984; German, 1974), 198.

10. Patrick D. Miller, Jr., "El, the Creator of Earth," *Bulletin of the American Schools of Oriental Research* 239 (Summer 1980): 43-46. Bruce Vawter ("Yahweh: Lord of the Heavens and the Earth," *Catholic Biblical Quarterly* 48, no. 3 [July 1986], 465f.) disputed Miller's contention and favored the translation of "Lord."

11. Raymond Abba ("Name," in the *Interpreter's Dictionary of the Bible* [Nashville: Abingdon Press, 1962], 3:505) offers the following statistics. Of 135 Old Testament names compounded with El, 22 are places or foreigners and 113 are personal Hebrew names.

12. Norman C. Habel (" 'Yahweh, Maker of Heaven and Earth': A Study in Traditional Criticism," *Journal of Biblical Literature* 91, no. 3 [September 1972]: 321-37), while representing the interplay between Canaanite and Yahwistic tradition, also stresses the discontinuity between the two.

13. See Gerhard von Rad, *Theologie des Alten Testaments*, 2 vols. (Munich: Chr. Kaiser Verlag, 1961), 1:32.

14. Lang, "Jahwe-allein," 49.

15. Gösta Ahlström, *Who Were the Israelites?* (Winona Lake, Ind.: Eisenbrauns, 1986), 94.

16. Bernhard W. Anderson, "God, OT view of," in *The Interpreter's Dictionary of the Bible* 3:427.

17. Morton Smith, "Religiöse Parteien bei den Israeliten vor 587," in *Der einzige Gott*, ed. B. Lang, (Munich: Kösel, 1981), 16-17.

18. See Bernhard Lang, *Wisdom and the Book of Proverbs: An Israelite Goddess Redefined* (New York: Pilgrim Press, 1986), 177ff.

19. Martin Noth, *Die israelitischen Personennamen im Rahmen der gemeinsemitischen Namengebung* (Stuttgart, 1928), 107-8.

20. Hermann Vorländer, "Der Monotheismus Israels als Antwort auf die Krise des Exils," in *Der einzige Gott*, ed. Lang, 100-101.

21. See Dennis J. McCarthy, "Exod 3:14: History, Philology and Theology," *Catholic Biblical Quarterly* 40, no. 3 (July 1978): 321.

22. J. Severino Croatto, "Yavé, el Dios de la 'presencia' salvífica: Ex. 3,14 en su contexto literario y querigmático," *Revista Bíblica* 43, no.3 (1981/3): 153-63.

23. One should of course be careful of too easy associations made between events as one perceives them and the qualities of God. "God's name is what God does" sounds nice, even profound. G. H. Parke-Taylor (*Yahweh: The Divine Name in the Bible* [Waterloo, Ont.: Wilfrid Laurier University Press, 1975], 11) repeats the phrase in citing Eliezer Berkovits. The question, however, always remains, exactly, "What *does* God do, and how does one know?"

24. A. Murtonen, *A Philological and Literary Treatise on the Old Testament Divine Names* (Helsinki, 1952), 80.

25. Remarkably, they are absent from Ezekiel and Trito-Isaiah.

26. Lorenzo Vigano (*Nomi e titoli di YHWH alla luce del semitico del Nordovest* [Rome: Biblical Institute Press, 1976]) discusses *adon* and other terms for God, as they may appear from texts hitherto unidentified before the advent of Northwest Semitic studies.

27. See Exodus 24; Isaiah 6; Ezekiel 1; Habakkuk 3.

28. Jörg Jeremias, *Theophanie: Die Geschichte einer alttestamentlichen Gattung* (Neukirchen-Vluyn: Erziehungsverein, 1965), 65 and esp. 112-15.

29. The question of the so-called impassibility of God will not be addressed here. It is quite clear that in the Old Testament, although it is several times flatly stated ("he is not a man, like me," Job 9:32) and everywhere assumed that God is not a human being, it is not only possible but natural to speak of God in anthropomorphical language which includes emotional as well as physiological features. Yet, never are emotions, or any other qualities, described of God which are evil, that is, contrary to God's own being; never is anything said of God to mean that God desires ultimate ill for creation.

30. Hans-Joachim Kraus, *Theology of the Psalms* (Minneapolis: Augsburg Publishing House, 1986; German, 1979), 41-46.

31. Norbert Lohfink (" 'Ich bin Jahwe, dein Arzt' (Ex 15,26)," in *"Ich will euer Gott werden," Beispiele biblischen Redens von Gott*, Stuttgarter Bibelstudien 100 [Stuttgart, 1981] offers something of a paradigmatic example of how a term may originate in literary and traditions-historical contexts.

32. Oskar Grether, *Name und Wort Gottes im Alten Testament* (Giessen: Alfred Töpelmann, 1934).

33. See Samuel Terrien, *The Elusive Presence: Toward a New Biblical Theology*, Religious Perspectives 26 (New York: Harper & Row, 1978).

34. Samuel E. Ballentine, *The Hidden God: The Hiding of the Face of God in the Old Testament*, Oxford Theological Monographs, (Oxford: Oxford University Press, 1983).

35. Ibid., 170.

36. Ibid., 161.

37. I would include Deut. 32:6; Jer. 3:4, 19; 31:9; Isa. 63:16; 64.8; and Mal. 2:10. In these passages "father" becomes virtually a title; in the many other passages commonly cited it is usually some fatherly function with which God is compared.

38. Or, "queen." See Urs Winter, *Frau und Göttin: Exegetische und ikonographische Studien zum weiblichen Gottesbild im Alten Israel und in dessen Umwelt* (Göttingen: Vandenhoeck & Ruprecht, 1983), "JHWH als 'Mutter,' " 535-38.

39. Beware of long lists of textual references! Is there another text besides Deut. 32:18 that specifically mentions both parents?

40. John W. Miller, "Depatriarchalizing God in Biblical Interpretation: A Critique," *Catholic Biblical Quarterly* 48, no. 4 (October 1986): 609-16.

41. Robert Hamerton-Kelly (*God the Father: Theology and Patriarchy in the Teaching of Jesus*, Overtures to Biblical Theology [Philadelphia: Fortress Press, 1979]) is helpful on this subject, esp. 43ff.

6. God in the New Testament

1. No short essay about God in the New Testament does comprehensive justice to the variety of language about God found there. This essay presents some aspects of New Testament God-talk to stimulate discussion about consequences for our language today.

2. See the excellent survey in John Ferguson, *The Religions of the Roman Empire, Aspects of Greek and Roman Life* (Ithaca, N. Y.: Cornell University Press, 1970), and André Marie Jean Festugiére's judiciously learned *Personal Religion Among the Greeks*, Sather Classical Lectures 26 (Berkeley and Los Angeles: University of California Press, 1954).

3. M. Tullius Cicero, *De natura deorum* 2.18-22 [47-59], ed. O. Plasberg (Leipzig: B. G. Teubner, 1917).

4. Augustine, *De civitale Dei* 2.

5. Ibid., 6.6-10.

6. See Aelius Aristides, *The Sacred Tales* I-VI (= Orations 47-52), in P. Aelius Aristides, *The Complete Works*, trans. Charles A. Behr (Leiden: E. J. Brill, 1981). 2.278-353. Behr's edition of the Greek text of *The Sacred Tales* is not yet published.

7. Apuleius, *Metamorphoses* 11. Latin text in Apuleius, *Metamorphoseon Libri XI*, ed. Rudolf Helm (Leipzig: B. G. Teubner, 1907), 266-91; English translation in Apuleius, *The Golden Ass* (London: Heinemann; New York: Putnam, 1919), 538-95.

8. See the "Hymn to Isis" from Cyme, *Bulletin de correspondance hellénique* 51 (1927): 379-80; translation in Frederick C. Grant, *Hellenistic Religions: The Age of Syncretism* (New York: Liberal Arts Press, 1953), 131-33; also in Marvin W. Meyer, ed., *The Ancient Mysteries: A Sourcebook* (San Francisco: Harper & Row, 1987), 172-74, R. E. Witt *(Isis in the Graeco-Roman World*, Aspects of Greek and Roman Life [Ithaca, N. Y.: Cornell University Press, 1971], 100-110) interprets the significance of these aretalogies.

9. The definitive modern study is Martin P. Nilsson, *The Dionysiac Mysteries of the Hellenistic and Roman Age*, Skrifter Utgivna av Svenska Institutet i Athen, no. 5 (Lund: C. W. K. Gleerup, 1957). Nilsson documents the vitality of this religion from texts and the body of surviving Dionysian art, e.g. the great fresco from the Villa of the Mysteries at Pompeii and the series of Dionysiac sarcophagi. See also Walter F. Otto, *Dionysus; Myth and Cult,* trans. Robert B. Palmer (Bloomington and London: Indiana University Press, 1965).

10. Robert M. Ogilvie, *The Romans and Their Gods in the Age of Augustus,* Ancient Culture and Society (London: Chatto & Windus, 1979).

11. See the convenient, generally accurate summary in Jerome Murphy-O'Connor, *St. Paul's Corinth: Texts and Archaeology,* Good News Studies 6 (Wilmington, Del.: Michael Glazier, 1983).

12. See the discussion of the dining facilities at Corinth in *Numina Aegaea* 2 (1975): 1-11 by Cynthia Thompson (cultic dining rooms; Asclepieion-Lerna Complex; theater caves at Isthmia [with Thomas Robinson] and Demeter sanctuary on Acrocorinth) and Dennis Smith (Egyptian cults, 12 pp.). Murphy-O'Connor calls attention to the size of the triclinium in the villa at Anaploga (Corinth) and in parallel houses at Pompeii and Olynthus to illuminate the problem of the agape feasts in house churches (1 Corinthians 11).

13. The Corinthians might have cited Paul's words in 1 Thess. 1:9-10 (if they knew them) to justify their claim: "how you turned from idols to a living and authentic God, and to await his Son." See Edgar Krentz, "Evangelism and Spirit: 1 Thessalonians 1," *Currents in Theology and Mission* 14 (1987): 22-30, esp. 25-26.

14. Paul's words do not make clear how he would respond to the claims that Isis is the creative force (cf. Cyme, *Isis Aretalogy*, 12-19).

15. Josephus, *Jewish War*, 5.438 (10.3).

16. Josephus, *Antiquities*, 2.275-76; English translation by H. St. John Thackeray in Loeb Classical Library, *Josephus*, 4:285 (emphasis mine).

17. Richard Wuensch, *Antike Fluchtafeln*, Kleine Texte 20, 2d ed. (Bonn: A. Marcus und E. Weber Verlag, 1912), 21-26. An English translation in G. Adolf Diessmann, *Bible Studies* (Edinburgh: T. & T. Clark, 1901), 273-300. A *tabula defixionis* is a lead table whose text seeks to compel a desired outcome (blessing or curse) through magic and the invoking of the proper god.

18. 1QS 6:27—7:2. The translation is from Geza Vermes, *The Dead Sea Scrolls in English* 2d ed. (New York: Penguin Books, 1975), 83. The Hebrew text is most conveniently available in Eduard Lohse, *Die Texte aus Qumran hebräisch und deutsch* (Darmstadt: Wissenschaftliche Buchgesellschaft, 1964), 28.

19. See Solomon A. Birnbaum, *The Qumran Scrolls and Palaeography*, Bulletin of the American Schools of Oriental Research, Supplementary Studies, nos. 13-14 (New Haven: American Schools of Oriental Research, 1952), 25-27 and Geza Vermes, *The Dead Sea Scrolls: Qumran in Perspective*, rev. ed. (Philadelphia: Fortress Press, 1981), 37, 42-43.

20. See the illustration of the Deuteronomy fragment (second century B.C.E.) in John C. Trevor's "Illustrated History of the Biblical Text," in *The Interpreter's Bible*, ed. George A. Buttrick et. al., 12 vols. (Abingdon Press, 1951-57), 12:628.

21. "In the more exact copies the name is given in Hebrew characters, not in the Hebrew ones of the present day, however, but in the ancient ones."

22. George Foot Moore, *Judaism in the First Centuries of the Christian Era: The Age of the Tannaim* (Cambridge: Harvard University Press, 1946), 1:428-29.

23. Gustav Dalman, *The Words of Jesus* (Edinburgh: T. & T. Clark, 1909, 179-234.

24. Translation by E. F. Scott, *The Lord's Prayer: Its Character, Purpose, and Interpretation* (New York: Charles Scribner's Sons, 1951), 41. Aramaic text in W. Staerk, *Altjüdische liturgische Gebete*, Kleine Texte, 58, 2d ed. (Berlin: Walter de Gruyter, 1930), 30.

25. Hebrew text in Staerk, *Altjüdische liturgische Gebete*, 11-14; English translation from Werner Foerster, *From the Exile to Christ* (Philadelphia: Fortress Press, 1964), 228-29.

26. Two passages have been omitted in the paragraph above. The doxology that concludes Romans 11 combines language from the Old Testament with the Stoic formula that ascribes God's priority to the created universe ("all things") in Rom. 11:36. Here alone in Romans, Paul comes close to Hellenistic philosophy in God-language. The doxology (Rom. 16:25-27) is not by Paul but was added at a later time, probably by a Marcionite writer. Cf. Ernst Käsemann, *Commentary on Romans* (Grand Rapids: Wm. B. Eerdmans, 1980), 421-28.

27. The most striking passage in the authentic Paulines is the berakah that opens 2 Corinthians. He is blessed as "the God and Father of our Lord Jesus Christ," which Paul then glosses with the phrase "the Father of mercies (*oiktirmōn*) and God of all comfort (*paraklēsis*), the one comforting us at every pressure"

(2 Cor. 1:3-4). "Father" is here given an interpretation that removes it from the simply genetic relationship to that of the forgiver and encourager. See 2 Cor. 5:20 for additional support.

28. *Tōi* makes of "God and Father" a single concept; it also functions as the possessive in this phrase.

29. Werner Georg Kümmel (*Introduction to the New Testament*, rev. ed. [Nashville and New York: Abingdon Press, 1975], 366) dates it between 80 and 100 C.E. Helmut Koester (*Introduction to the New Testament*, vol. 2: *History and Literature of Early Christianity* [Philadelphia: Fortress Press: Berlin and New York: Walter de Gruyter, 1982], 2:268) dates it shortly after 100 C.E. on the basis of its anti-gnostic language. The lack of apocalyptic language, in my opinion, favors the 80s; there was a resurgence of apocalyptic in the 90s, especially in Asia Minor and Greece, as 2 Thessalonians and the Apocalypse of John suggest. See Koester *Introduction to the New Testament*, 2:241-57.

30. G. Kittel, in Gerhard Kittel and Gerhard Friedrich, eds., *Theological Dictionary of the New Testament*, trans. Geoffrey Bromiley, 10 vols. (Grand Rapids: Wm. B. Eerdmans, 1964-76), 1:6, s.v. *Abba*.

31. Hans-Joachim Kraus, "Der lebendige Gott: Ein Kapitel biblischer Theologie," *Evangelische Theologie* 27 (1967): 169-200. Kraus calls attention to other New Testament passages that reflect the formula: Acts 14:15, Rom. 9:26; 14:11; 1 Thess. 1:9; and 2 Cor. 3:3; 6:16.

32. My colleague Wilhelm Linss pointed out that almost all of these occur in citations from the Old Testament in the phrase "the angel of the Lord," or in the phrase "said through the Lord," used to introduce citations from the Old Testament.

33. Matt. 6:8, 15; 10:20, 29; 11:25, 26, 27 (tris); 13:43; 16:27; 24:36; 26:29, 39, 42, 53; 28:19.

34. Matt. 5:16, 45; 6:1, 9; 7:11, 21; 10:32, 33; 12:50; 16:17; 18:10, 14, 19; 19:12, 14. Adolf Schlatter called attention to a significant linguistic feature in the use of the term "heaven." He argues that the Septuagint, Josephus, Philo, and Matthew used the plural ("heavens," *ouranoi*) when heaven is conceived of as completely different from earth, as the special seat and home of God; cf. the address in the Lord's Prayer in Matt. 6:9: "Our Father, the One in the Heavens." The singular emphasizes the closeness of earth and heaven as the correlative parts of God's created universe; cf. the third petition, "Your will be done, as in heaven [singular], so also on earth" (Matt. 6:10). See Adolf Schlatter, *Die Theologie des Judentums nach dem Bericht des Josefus* (Gütersloh: Bertelsmann, 1932), 8.

35. No other writer of the New Testament applies the adjective *ouranios* to the Father!

36. See Edgar Krentz, "Community and Character: Matthew's Vision of the Church," *Society of Biblical Literature 1987 Seminar Papers* (Atlanta: Scholars Press, 1987), 565-73.

37. Robert Hamerton-Kelly, *God the Father: Theology and Patriarchy in the Teaching of Jesus,* Overtures to Biblical Theology (Philadelphia: Fortress Press, 1979), 89-90.

38. More adequately called teaching on piety.

39. "God" is completely absent from John 2; 14; 15; and 18, a phenomenon for which I have no explanation at present.

40. A cursory reading of 1 John shows that it stands in the same tradition.

41. James M. Reese, "The Principal Model of God in the New Testament," *Biblical Theology Bulletin* 8 (1978): 126-31.

42. Reprinted in Karl Holl, *Gesammelte Aufsätze zur Kirchengeschichte*, Vol. 2: *Der Osten* (Tübingen: J. C. B. Mohr [Paul Siebeck], 1928), 1-32. It was translated into English by Norman V. Hope and published as a separate monograph under the title *The Distinctive Elements in Christianity* (Edinburgh: T. & T. Clark, 1937).

43. Rudolph Bultmann, "Urchristentum und Religionsgeschichte," (*Theologische Rundschau*) (1932): 1-21.

44. I owe this interesting collection of articles to Gerhard Lohfink, "Gott in der Verkündigung Jesu," in *Heute von Gott reden*, ed. Martin Hengel and Rudolf Reinhardt (Munich: Chr. Kaiser Verlag; Mainz: Grünewald, 1977), 50.

45. Rudolf Bultmann, *New Testament Theology* (New York: Charles Scribner's Sons, 1951), 1:3-32.

46. See Joachim Jeremias, "Abba," in *The Prayers of Jesus* (London: SCM Press, 1967) 11-65, and idem, *New Testament Theology: The Proclamation of Jesus* (New York: Charles Scribner's Sons, 1971), 178-203.

47. Hans-Peter Rüger was able to locate only six instances in rabbinic literature where the Aramaic term is used of God ("Aramaisch II. Im Neuen Testament," *Theologische Realenzyklopädie*, 3:602-3).

48. Lohfink ("Gott in der Verkündigung Jesu," 55-56) stresses that *abba* has an intimate, familiar, everyday, almost profane tone. It contradicts the attitude of the first benediction of the Shemoneh Esreh.

49. See Israel Abrahams, "VII. Publicans and Sinners," in *Studies in Pharisaism and the Gospels* (Cambridge: Cambridge University Press, 1917; New York Ktav, 1967), First Series, 54-61.

50. Thus the Thessalonians are called to faith in "a living and authentic God, and to await his Son from the heavens, whom he raised from the dead, Jesus, the one rescuing us from the wrath that is on the way" (1 Thess. 1:9-10). The resurrection demonstrates that he is a living and authentic God and shows that he is Jesus' Father.

51. See Robert Jewett, *Christian Tolerance: Paul's Message to the Modern Church* (Philadelphia: Westminster Press, 1982), 36-42.

52. Leander E. Keck, "Toward the Renewal of New Testament Christology," *New Testament Studies* 32 (1986): 363.

7. Putting the Nature of God into Language: Naming the Trinity

1. Friedrich Schleiermacher, *The Christian Faith*, trans. H. R. Mackintosh and J. S. Stewart, 2d ed. (Edinburgh: T. & T. Clark, 1928), 170, 2:739-40.

2. The protracted debates over whether the Trinity is "essential" or only "revelational," "immanent" or only "economic," are hereby given short shrift in a single paragraph, not to depreciate their seriousness, although the former distinction does seem misplaced, especially if it reads back into God (as it threatens to in the theologies of Schleiermacher and Albrecht Ritschl) the Kantian distinction be-

tween "things in themselves" and "appearances." For a handy overview of recent literature, see Ted Peter, "Trinity Talk: Part I," *Dialog* 26 (1987): 44-48. A notable advance in the debate is Wolfhart Pannenberg, "Problems of a Trinitarian Doctrine of God," trans. Philip Clayton, *Dialog* 26 (1987): 250-57.

3. Martin Luther, *Werke,* Kirtische Gesamtausgabe, Weimarer Ausgabe (Weimar: Boehlau, 1883 to the present), 38:612.

4. Raymond E. Brown, *Jesus, God and Man* (New York: Macmillan Co., 1967); J. A. Fitzmyer, *A Christological Catechism* (New York: Paulist Press, 1982), 43-48, 82-93, Reginald H. Fuller, *The Foundations of New Testament Christology* (New York: Charles Scribner's Sons, 1965); Martin Hengel, *The Son of God,* trans. John Bowden (Philadelphia: Fortress Press, 1976); and Edward Schillebeeckx, *Jesus: An Experiment in Christology,* trans. Hubert Hoskins (London: William Collins Sons, 1979).

5. A. Kelly, "Trinity and Process, Relevance of the Basic Christian Confession of God," *Theological Studies* 31 (1970): 393-414; Lewis S. Ford, "Process Trinitarianism," *Journal of the American Academy of Religion* 43 (1975): 199-213; Norman Pittenger, "Trinity and Process: Some Comments and a Reply," *Theological Studies* 32 (1971): 290-96; and P. Schoonenberg, "Process or History in God," *Theological Digest* 23 (1975): 38-44.

6. Joan Chamberlain Engelsmann, *The Feminine Dimension of the Divine* (Philadelphia: Westminster Press, 1979), 139.

7. Valerie Saiving, "The Human Situation: A Feminine View," reprinted in *Womanspirit Rising* ed. Carol P. Christ and Judith Plaskow (New York: Harper & Row, 1979), 25-42.

8. For recent discussions of Tillich's "method of correlation" which are pertinent also to the concerns of this essay, see Francis Schüssler Fiorenza, *Foundational Theology: Jesus and the Church* (New York: Crossroad, 1984), 276-84; Rosemary Radford Ruether, "Feminist Interpretation: A Method of Correlation," in *Feminist Interpretation of the Bible* ed. Letty M. Russell (Philadelphia: Westminster Press, 1985), 111-24; Ronald Thiemann, *Revelation and Theology* (Notre Dame, Ind.: University of Notre Dame Press, 1985), 186-88; and David Tracy, "Particular Questions with General Concerns," in *Consensus in Theology* ed. Leonard Swidler (Philadelphia: Westminster Press, 1980), 33-39.

9. The book that in English has perhaps been most used recently to provide a trinitarian basis for a communitarian ethic is Jürgen Moltmann, *The Trinity and the Kingdom* trans. Margaret Kohl (New York: Harper & Row, 1981).

10. See the article "Augustine, St., Doctor of the Church," in *Trinitas: A Theological Encyclopedia of the Holy Trinity* by Michael O'Carroll, (Wilmington, Del.: Michael Glazier, 1987), 42-45; E. Cousins, "A Theology of Interpersonal Relations," *Thought,* 45 (1970): 56-82; and Wolfhart Pannenberg, *Jesus—God and Man* trans. Lewis Wilkins and Duane Priebe (Philadelphia: Westminster Press, 1968), 180-83.

11. Barbara Brown Zikmund, "The Trinity and Women's Experience," *The Christian Century* 104 (1987): 356.

12. Ibid.

13. A similar claim is argued, not altogether unsympathetically with liberalism, in Robert Bertram, "A Smithian Luther and Faith-based Universalism," unpublished essay presented at the Lewis Conference on "The Future of Christian Theology in a Threatened World," Saint Louis University, 19 October 1985.

14. Not that that the *de facto* situation of "unfaith," as Tracy calls it, is not deplored. On the contrary, it means the "failure to live a human life," "demanding nothing short of conversion to the commitment to actualize that common basic faith." And what if, as in fact seems to be the case on a wide scale, "such persons—inside and outside the churches"—do not realize such "conversion to the commitment"? For all of Tracy's "hesitancy" about process theism's "fellow sufferer," about "warm deism," his theology of God seems limited to the same traditional option of liberalism: finding a more adequate symbolic "re-presentation" of "God's persuasive . . . power of love," as though the only alternative to "persuasive" were "coercive." Might not another alternative be for our "unfaith" and "failure" to be "re-presented" as God the Child's own heroic and consummate faith "for us"? David Tracy, *Blessed Rage for Order* (New York: Seabury Press, 1975), 153ff., 186-87.

15. Karl Barth, *Church Dogmatics* trans. G. W. Bromiley et al. (New York: Charles Scribner's Sons, 1956ff.), II/2:52f.; II/1:18f.; IV/2:50f.; II/1:26; IV/1:210.

16. Karl Barth, *The Humanity of God*, trans. J. N. Thomas and Thomas Wieser (Richmond, Va.: John Knox Press, 1960), 46-55.

17. Barth, *Church Dogmatics*, II/1:503-4; II/2:165-66; III/3:349-52, 357-59; IV/3:538-49; and Karl Barth, "An Introductory Essay," trans. J. L. Adams, in Ludwig Feuerbach *The Essence of Christianity* trans. George Eliot (New York: Harper & Row, Torchbooks, 1957), xxii-xxv.

18. Ibid.

19. Cited in J. N. D. Kelly, *Early Christian Doctrines* (New York: Harper & Brothers, 1958), 227.

20. J. N. D. Kelly, *Early Christian Creeds* (London: Longmans, 1960), 148.

21. Athanasius, *Orations Against the Arians*, in *The Trinitarian Controversy* trans. and ed. W. G. Rusch (Philadelphia: Fortress Press, 1980), 76-77.

22. Ibid., 67-68.

23. Ibid., 100-104.

24. Ibid., 109, 119, 102.

25. Ibid., 107, 104.

26. Ibid., 104-5.

27. Formula of Concord 8:85 in *The Book of Concord*, trans. and ed. Theodore Tappert (Philadelphia: Fortress Press, 1959), 608.

28. Dorothy L. Sayers, "The Shattering Dogmas of the Christian Tradition," in *Christian Letters to a Post-Christian World* (Grand Rapids: Wm. B. Eerdmans, 1969), 14.

29. Athanasius, *Orations*, in *The Trinitarian Controversy*, trans. and ed. Rusch, 102, 104, 115.

30. Ibid., 105-6, 109.

31. Formula of Concord 8:96, in *The Book of Concord*, trans. and ed. Tappert, 610.

32. Gregory of Nyssa, *Concerning We Should Not Think of Saying That There Are Not Three Gods, To Ablabius,* in *The Trinitarian Controversy,* trans. and ed. Rusch, 160; and J. N. D. Kelly, *Early Christian Doctrines,* 264-65.

33. J. N. D. Kelly, *Early Christian Doctrines,* and Gregory of Nyssa, *Concerning We Should Not Think of Saying That There Are Not Three Gods,* in *The Trinitarian Controversy,* trans. and ed. Rusch, 155.

34. Gregory of Nazianzus, *Third Theological Oration Concerning the Son* in *The Trinitarian Controversy,* trans. and ed. Rusch, 144.

35. Ibid.

36. Ibid., 146.

37. J. N. D. Kelly, *Early Christian Doctrines,* 297.

38. Ibid.

39. Cyril of Alexandria, *Second Letter to Nestorius,* in *The Christological Controversy,* ed. Richard A. Norris, Jr. (Philadelphia: Fortress Press, 1980), 134, 133.

40. Nestorius, *Second Letter to Cyril,* trans. and ed. Richard A. Norris, Jr., in *The Christological Controversy,* ed. Norris, 138.

41. Ibid., 139, 136.

42. Quoted in Cyril Alexandria, *Letter to John of Antioch,* in *The Christological Controversy,* ed. Norris, 142; and the Council of Chalcedon, *Definition of the Faith* in *The Christological Controversy* ed. Norris, 159.

43. Anne Wilson Schaef, *Co-Dependence: Misunderstood-Mistreated* (Minneapolis: Winston Press, 1986).

44. Sandra M. Schneiders, *Women and the Word* (New York: Paulist Press, 1986), 70-71. Similarly, Gail Ramshaw-Schmidt, 'De Divinis Nominibus: The Gender of God," in *The Word and Words: Beyond Gender in Theological and Liturgical Language,* ed. William D. Watley (Princeton, N. J.: Consultation on Church Union, 1983), "Change of speech is a willing task if it follows a conversion of mind," 24.

45. For an elaboration of this description of the Holy Spirit, see Robert Bertram, "Constructive Lutheran Theology of the Saints," unpublished essay presented to the Lutheran-Roman Catholic Consultation U.S.A., in Burlingame, Calif., 22 February 1986.

46. On the issue of a feminized pneumatology, pro and con, see Susan Brooks Thistlethwaite, *Metaphors for the Contemporary Church* (New York: Pilgrim Press, 1983), 101-29; also George Tavard, "Sexist Language in Theology?" in *Woman: New Dimensions,* ed. Walter J. Burghardt (New York: Paulist Press, 1975), 124-48. These two works I find largely convincing. Not so, Leonard Swidler, "God the Father: Masculine; God the Son: Masculine; God the Holy Spirit: Feminine," *National Catholic Reporter,* 31 January 1975, 7 and 14. The rule that seems most persuasive, though difficult to practice in an essay (like the present one) on the tradition of the Trinity, is that of Gail Ramshaw-Schmidt: "God the Spirit as 'she' is unacceptable not because our God ends up only one-third female, but because we must speak of God with the highest accuracy possible, and God is neither . . . he nor she. Yet there are occasions when 'she' can be used metaphorically in the naming of God. Use of 'she' immediately indicates the inadequacy of 'he' " (Ramshaw-Schmidt, "De Divinis Nominibus," in *The Word and Words,* ed. Watley, 23).

47. Matt. 16:17; Luke 10:21-22; 17:30; John 12:37-41; 1 Cor. 2:10; Gal. 1:16; 1 Peter 4:13.

48. Augsburg Confession 1:6, in *The Book of Concord*, ed. Tappert, 28.

49. J. N. D. Kelly, *Early Christian Doctrines*, 265, 275.

50. A succinct statement of that demonstration is Schneiders's *Women and the Word*, 20ff. On the other hand, the sobering reminder is still in order that patriarchalism not only appears in Scripture but is taught there. Elisabeth Schüssler Fiorenza, *Bread Not Stone* (Boston: Beacon Press, 1984), esp. 65-92.

51. Joachim Jeremias, *The Central Message of the New Testament* (New York: Charles Scribner's Sons, 1965); Mary Collins, "Naming God in Public Prayer," *Worship* 59 (1985): 291-304; Robert Hamerton-Kelly, *God the Father: Theology and Patriarchy in the Teaching of Jesus*, Overtures to Biblical Theology (Philadelphia: Fortress Press, 1979).

52. Diane Tennis, *Is God the Only Reliable Father?* (Philadelphia: Westminster Press, 1985).

53. Stanley Kunitz, "The Poet's Quest for the Father," *New York Times Book Review*, 22 February 1987, 37.

54. Quoted in the article 'Problem,' The Trinitarian," in *Trinitas: A Theological Encyclopedia*, by O'Carroll, 188.

8. Missiological Naming: "Who Shall I Say Sent Me?"

1. W. A. Visser 't Hooft, *No Other Name: The Choice Between Syncretism and Christian Universalism* (London: SCM Press, 1963).

2. Paul Knitter, *No Other Name? A Critical Survey of Christian Attitudes Toward the World Religions* (Maryknoll, N. Y.: Orbis Books, 1985).

3. See *Mission Studies*, Journal of the International Association for Mission Studies, vol. III-1 and 2 (1986), no. 5, pp. 51-60, and no. 6, pp. 64-84.

4. David Bosch, "Toward a Hermeneutic for 'Biblical Studies and Mission,'" *Mission Studies*, vol. III-2, no. 6 (1986): 65-66.

5. Walter E. Brueggemann, "The Bible and Mission: Some Interdisciplinary Implications for Teaching," *Missiology* 10, no 4. (October 1982): 397-98.

6. Ibid., 410.

7. Robert Schreiter, "The Bible in Mission: A Response to Walter Brueggemann and Beverly Gaventa," *Missiology* 10, no. 4 (October 1982): 432.

8. Data are taken from Gerhard Kittel and Gerhard Friedrich, eds., *Theological Dictionary of the New Testament*, trans. Geoffrey W. Bromiley; abridged in one volume by Geoffrey W. Bromiley (Grand Rapids: Wm. B. Eerdmans, 1985). See the article on *onoma*, 694-700; on *apostellō, pempō, apostolos*, 67-74; and on *poreuomai*, 915-16. Various concordances have also been consulted.

9. Doxology and the Trinity

1. Gail Ramshaw, "Liturgy as Poetry: Implications of a Definition," *Living Worship* 15, no. 8 (October 1979) 2-3.

2. See Gail Ramshaw-Schmidt, *Christ in Sacred Speech* (Philadelphia: Fortress Press, 1986). See also Sallie McFague, *Metaphorical Theology: Models of God in Religious Language* (Philadelphia: Fortress Press, 1982), 31-66.

3. See W. H. Auden, "Art and the Christian," in *The Dyer's Hand, and Other Essays*, by W. H. Auden (New York: Vintage Books, 1968); Sister M. Bernetta Quinn, O.S.F., "What Poetry Makes Happen," *Response* 8, no. 4 (1967) 196-203 (a response to Auden's odd valediction of Yeats); Jay C. Rochelle, "Surplus and Surface, *Dialogue* 25, no. 4 (Fall 1986): 266-71; and Daniel B. Stevick, "The Language of Prayer," *Response* 16, no. 3 (1976): 5-18.

4. Dietrich Bonhoeffer, *Life Together*, trans. John W. Doberstein (New York: Harper & Brothers, 1954), chap. 1, esp. 21-27; and idem, *Christ the Center*, new trans. by Edwin H. Robertson (New York: Harper & Row, 1978), p. 1, 43-65.

5. Cf., e.g., the invitation to the table and the formula for distribution in the *Book of Common Prayer* (1978 ed.), 338.

6. See Harvey H. Guthrie, Jr., *Theology as Thanksgiving* (New York: Seabury Press, 1981); Robert Ledogar, "The Eucharistic Prayer and the Gifts Over Which It Is Spoken," in *Living Bread, Saving Cup*, ed. R. Kevin Seasoltz, (Collegeville, Minn.: Liturgical Press, 1982), 60-79. We would not wish to be misunderstood; there are many transitions from *berakah* to *eucharistia*. The Christian prayers are not simply adaptations of their Jewish textual antecedents; cf. Thomas Talley, "From *Berakah* to *Eucharistia*: A Reopening Question," in *Living Bread, Saving Cup*, ed. Seasoltz. Talley's chief contention is that the pattern of benediction–thanksgiving–supplication is possibly to safeguard the distinction between God the Creator/Father and Jesus Christ the Redeemer. Talley is quite sure this shift in pattern enables future eucharistic prayers to assume their characteristic trinitarian shape; cf. 94ff., esp. 100-101.

7. Josef A. Jungmann, *The Early Liturgy to the Time of Gregory the Great* (Notre Dame, Ind.: University of Notre Dame Press, 1959), 190ff.

8. Ibid, 296-98; citation, 298.

9. Eastern orthodoxy is the obvious case in point; cf. *inter alia* such classics as Vladimir Lossky, *The Mystical Theology of the Eastern Church* (London: James Clarke & Co., 1968); idem, *The Vision of God*, 2d ed. (Leighton Buzzard, Bedfordshire: Faith Press, 1973); and Leonid Ouspensky, *Theology of the Icon* (Crestwood, N. Y.: St. Vladimir's Seminary Press, 1978). For brief introductions, see "A Monk of the Eastern Church" (Lev Gillet), *Orthodox Spirituality* (London: SPCK 1968), esp. 22-40; Archbishop Paul of Finland, *The Faith We Hold* (Crestwood, N. Y.: St. Vladimir's Seminary Press, 1980), 65-90; and Kallistos Ware, *The Orthodox Way* (Crestwood, N. Y.: St. Vladimir's Seminary Press, 1985).

10. Geoffrey Wainwright, *Doxology: The Praise of God in Worship, Doctrine, and Life* (New York: Oxford University Press, 1980), 3.

11. Dietrich Ritschl, *Memory and Hope* (New York: Macmillan Co., 1967), is a good study of the concept of memory in Christian faith; see also idem, *The Logic of Theology* (Philadelphia: Fortress Press, 1987), 44-65 and 239-85. I have found Ritschl's work very helpful for many years.

12. Markus Barth, *Jesus the Jew* (Atlanta: John Knox Press, 1978), 11-40; Charlotte Klein, *Anti-Judaism in Christian Theology* (Philadelphia: Fortress Press, 1978); and Rosemary Radford Ruether, *Faith and Fratricide* (New York: Seabury Press, 1974) are primary resources. For a reasonably good discussion of the God-

issues, see Pinchas Lapide and Jürgen Moltmann, *Jewish Monotheism and Christian Trinitarian Doctrine* (Philadelphia: Fortress Press, 1981).

13. Wainwright, *Doxology*, 11, 45-70.

14. Boris Bobrinsky, "Revelation of the Spirit: Language beyond Words," *Sobornost* 8 no. 1 (1986), 13.

15. Wainwright, *Doxology*, 7.

16. Gerald Sloyan, "The Creeds: The Apostles' Creed," *Pace* 13 (Winona, Minn.: St. Mary's Press, 1982-83), 4, and idem, "The Creeds: The Ecumenical Creed of East and West," ibid, 5. See also Wainwright, *Doxology*, 182-98.

17. On liturgical catechesis, consult Mary Pierre Ellebracht, *The Easter Passage: The RCIA Experience* (Minneapolis: Winston Press, 1983); Owen Kennedy Neville and John H. Westerhoff III, *Learning Through Liturgy* (New York: Seabury Press, 1978); Mark Searle, *Christening: The Making of Christians* (Collegeville Pa.: Liturgical Press, 1980); and Robert Webber, *Celebrating Our Faith* (New York: Harper & Row, 1986). The Roman Catholics publish a journal especially devoted to liturgical catechesis called *Catechumenate* (Chicago: Liturgy Training Publications).

18. Ignatius of Antioch, *Letter to the Ephesians, Letter to the Magnesians, and Letter to the Romans,* in *Early Christian Fathers*, ed. Cyril C. Richardson, Library of Christian Classics, vol. 1 (Philadelphia: Westminster Press, 1953), 1:87-97, 102-6.

19. Thomas Talley, "The Eucharistic Prayer: Tradition and Development," in *Liturgy Reshaped*, by Kenneth Stevenson, (London: SPCK, 1982) 48ff.

20. See Guthrie, *Theology as Thanksgiving*, esp. 145-180.

21. On Jewish Pentecost, see Peter S. Knobel, ed., *Gates of the Seasons: A Guide to the Jewish Year* (New York: Central Conference of American Rabbis, 1983), 65-74; and Hayylm Schauss, *The Jewish Festivals: History and Observance* (NewYork: Schocken Books, 1938), 38-85, On Christian Pentecost, see Adolf Adam, *The Liturgical Year* (New York: Pueblo Press, 1981), 84-91; Jay C. Rochelle, *The Revolutionary Year* (Philadelphia: Fortress Press, 1973), 63-74, and, idem, "Four Cycles of Ritual in Christian Observance," 357-62, *Currents in Theology and Mission* 11, no. 6 (December 1984); and Thomas Talley, *The Origins of the Liturgical Year* (New York: Pueblo Press, 1986), 57-65.

22. Justin Martyr, *Dialogue with Trypho* 117.5 in *The Eucharist of the Early Christians*, by Willy Rordorf and others (New York: Pueblo Press, 1978), 78.

23. Cited in A. Hamman, ed., *Early Christian Prayers* (Chicago: Henry Regnery Co., 1961), 103.

24. Ledogar, "The Eucharistic Prayer," in *Living Bread*, ed. Seasoltz, 62.

25. Joseph A. Sittler, "Dogma and Doxa," in *Worship: Good News in Action,* ed. Mandus. A. Egge, (Minneapolis: Augsburg Publishing House, 1973), 7-23.

26. Ledogar, "The Eucharistic Prayer," in *Living Bread*, ed. Seasoltz, 63.

27. Text in Richardson, *Early Christian Fathers*, 171-82; commentary in ibid., 161ff., and Rordorf, *The Eucharist of the Early Christians*, 1-23.

28. Text in Richardson, *Early Christian Fathers*, 242-89; commentary in ibid., 225ff, and Rordorf, *The Eucharist of the Early Christians*, 71-85.

29. For further information, consult Lucien Deiss, *Springtime of the Liturgy* (Collegeville, Pa.: Liturgical Press, 1967); Hamman, *Early Christian Prayers;* Rich-

ardson, *Early Christian Fathers;* Rordorf, *The Eucharist of the Early Christians;* and
for the overall history, cf. Theodor Klauser, *A Short History of the Western Liturgy*
(New York: Oxford University Press, 1979); William D. Maxwell, *An Outline of
Christian Worship* (London: Oxford University Press, 1960); Herman Wegman,
Christian Worship in East and West (New York: Pueblo Press, 1986). Of course, the
classic work in the development of liturgy remains, for the most part, Dom
Gregory Dix, *The Shape of the Liturgy* (London: Dacre Press, 1945).

30. Ambrose of Milan, *De Sacramentis* 4.5.25.

31. Sources abound in this area also. See, among others, Dietrich Bonhoeffer,
Spiritual Care (Philadelphia: Fortress Press, 1985); Kenneth Leech, *Spirituality
and Pastoral Care* (London: Sheldon Press, 1986); Elaine Ramshaw, *Ritual and
Pastoral Care* (Philadelphia: Fortress Press, 1987); Jay C. Rochelle, "Liturgy and
Therapy," *Vox*, Winter 1986; and William Willimon, *Worship and Pastoral Care*
(Nashville: Abingdon Press, 1983).

32. Robertson Davies, *What's Bred in the Bone* (New York: Penguin Books,
1985), 124 (italics mine).

33. See the brilliant introduction by Jean Daniélou to *From Glory to Glory*,
trans. Herbert Musurillo (Crestwood, N. Y.: St. Vladimir's Seminary Press, 1979),
3-78.

34. Gregory of Nyssa, *The Life of Moses*, trans. A. Malherbe, (New York: Paulist Press, 1978).

35. George A. Maloney, S.J., ed., *Pilgrimage of the Heart* (New York: Harper &
Row, 1983), 178-79.

36. Pseudo-Macarius, *The Spiritual Homilies* (Denville, N. J.: Dimension
Books, 1978), homily 44, p. 205.

37. Ledogar, "The Eucharistic Prayer," in *Living Bread*, ed. Seasoltz, 60ff.; also
Kenneth Stevenson, " 'Ye shall pray for . . .': The Intercession," in *Liturgy Reshaped*, by Stevenson, 32-47.

38. See Geoffrey Wainwright, *Eucharist and Eschatology* (New York: Oxford
University Press, 1981).

39. Albert Schweitzer, *The Quest of the Historical Jesus* (New York: Macmillan
Paperback, 1961.

40. Dix, *The Shape of the Liturgy*.

41. Casel's work is most accessible in Louis Bouyer, *Liturgical Piety* (Notre
Dame, Ind.: University of Notre Dame Press, 1955), 86-98, and critiques from a
Lutheran perspective by Robert W. Jenson, *Visible Words* (Philadelphia: Fortress
Press, 1978), 73-77.

42. *Baptism, Eucharist and Ministry* (Geneva: World Council of Churches Faith
and Order Paper no. 111, 1982); Max Thurian, ed., *Ecumenical Perspectives on
Baptism, Eucharist and Ministry* (Geneva: World Council of Churches Faith and
Order Paper No. 116, 1983); Max Thurian, ed., *Churches Resond to BEM, Volume
III* (Geneva: World Council of Churches Faith and Order Paper no. 135, 1987).

43. *Baptism, Eucharist and Ministry*, sec. E, pars. 22 and 26, pp. 14 and 15.

44. Ibid.